I DIED TO REMEMBER

DEATH is not the end
        it is simply a shift in focus

LIFE is an ETERNAL EXPRESSION
        of the infinite LOVE LIGHT

By Mary V. McMurray, Ph.D.

MALLARD PUBLISHING
TRAVERSE CITY, MICHIGAN

I DIED TO REMEMBER

Death is not the end

By Mary V. McMurray, Ph.D.

Published by: **MALLARD PUBLISHING**
Post Office Box 82-P
Traverse City, Michigan
49685-0082

Library of Congress Cataloging in Publication Data
McMurray, Mary V., Ph.D.
I DIED TO REMEMBER: Death is not an end
CIP 91-90568
ISBN 0-9630230-0-4 : $9.95 Softcover

CONTENTS

PREFACE

This book had to be written. I couldn't sleep until it was, no matter how creatively I tried to put it off. I was repeatedly guided back to it. My resistance to putting these words on paper comes from the fact that much of what I want to share is actually indescribable with words. I have written before and with much more ease than I write this work, but I feel I am compelled to make my best effort at sharing a profound experience and its impact with you.

Other professionals before me have expertly written about the subject of near-death-experiences (NDEs) from the perspective of a scientist/clinician writing about a collection of case studies. The material in print offered by both Melvin Morse, M.D., and Raymond A. Moody, Jr., M.D. is extremely valuable. For myself personally, their putting into print other case studies of near-death-experiences has given me the courage to write this manuscript.

In I DIED TO REMEMBER I am writing from the first person position about a very personal experience. However, I am also including input from my professional self as a Counseling Psychologist/Human Resource Developer.

It is not my intention to convince anyone to adopt my perspective. I do not wish to engage in debating or defending any part of my manuscript. This is my personal story - not a sermon - not a theory - only a personal sharing handled with my best professional integrity. I agree with Dr. Wayne Dyer when he said that he has reached a point in his life when "it really doesn't matter if others think you're crazy.

Millions in the United States alone have had near-death-experiences similar to the one I am writing about. Millions more have had spiritual awakening experiences that are somewhat similar to a near-death-experience. It is my hope that to some this book will be comforting, when they see their own story in print. To others it may lessen the fear of the unknown. In any case, I hope that my efforts are useful to many.

If reading this material brings the reader to a more peaceful, loving life, then my labor has born abundant fruit. If not, then I have personally set myself free by being courageous enough to stand up and say what I think and feel without worry of public response. In either situation, the universe benefits. I do have the interest of all mankind in my heart as I share with you the following pages in the name of Love.

It is my hope that the following pages are enjoyable reading. I have purposely not used clinical jargon. I've written in a conversational style I sincerely hope will be appreciated by many. You will also find that I use the terms LOVE and ALMIGHTY CREATIVE POWER interchangeably. So if I neglect to print both terms consistently please consider getting into the habit of reading/thinking both terms when one or the other is written. This practice will help you to understand more clearly what I mean.

The form the book takes is a collection of essays. The first one describes the actual death experience. Following are several sets of ideas and topics that are a reflection of how the experience has affected my way of living, working, and looking at life. I am discussing in each essay the topic/idea as if seen from the perspective I was in while dead (or outside this specific physical reality). My perspective is as if I am standing on a mountain top where I could see in all directions infinitely and simultaneously. Although I am writing these words with the utmost of conscience, please keep in mind that it is through this human vessel that I am interpreting the Almighty Creative Power/Love energy.

Through life experiences, and in my professional work as a trainer and therapist, I realize that we all say and hear the same words through our own personal interpretive systems. There are occasions when a statement means totally different things to different people. If there is anything said here that confuses, or challenges you, I would enjoy hearing from you.

What I write on these pages is expressed through my human system at its current developmental stage, and I reserve the right to grow into more and more clarity on any subject discussed in this book. I offer respect of personal ideas to every other living thing, and I appreciate that respect in return. Thank you.

ACKNOWLEDGEMENTS

It would become a book itself to express the endless gratitude owed to those who have helped and supported me with their time, expertise, feedback, resources, financial help, and guidance of many and various kinds. To name a few there's Lisa, Tina, Cheryl, Larry, Sherry, Raggs, Alice, Dan, John, Bruce, Ernie, Jim, Victoria, Barb, Mom, Vel, Pat, Dave, Adam, and Eleanore. Thank you one and all!

Most of all, I would like to thank my husband, Jerry, for his very loving emotional support, his constant encouragement, and especially his acceptance of my work on this project. Thank you sweetheart. The following poem is dedicated to you.

My Gift To You

The best I can give you is me.

The real me, not the roles I play,

   but the me inside -

     the sensitive, vulnerable me.

I must trust you to let you love me,

   and to love you back.

Having trust, allows me to risk sharing

   the real, unmasked me with you.

My gift to you Love is ME.

"I have loved you with an everlasting love;
I have drawn you with loving kindness."

Jeremiah 31:5

DYING

I sat in the comfortable plush seat of my luxury car in the south exit of a Shell gas station. On a cold February day in a north midwestern city, I looked to my left and saw a wet slippery vacant westbound road with patches of snow here and there. I looked to my right and saw an opening in the moderate traffic heading eastbound, the direction I desired to go. I lifted my foot from the brake and allowed my car to begin rolling across the westbound lanes slowly so that I could steer into an open position heading east. I looked once more to my left and my eyes froze on the vision of a little white sports car flying into my driver's door. F-i-e-r-o were the letters printed on the car's hood that pressed deeply into my space as I howled at impact.

Instantly I found my consciousness experiencing myself in green fields, on paths, on a dirt road, on a highway and various other places just as real as the one I'd left. Moving from one place or space in time was as

11

simple as shifting my focus ever so slightly.
The shift was as slight as the thinness of the
edge of onion skin paper. It felt as though
each time-space were superimposed upon the
others, all in the same place simultaneously.
And all I had to do was to focus on whatever
one I wanted. With each shift in focus I was
totally a part of that reality. I don't know
how long this went on because time was distort-
ed or irrelevant or non-existent, but it felt
brief even though it also felt infinite in the
awareness I was experiencing.

Then my focus went back to the time and
space of being in the car in which I was com-
pressed between the door and console. The
frame had been bent in two and one-half (2 1/2)
feet and against the transmission hump. I
couldn't move anything except my head, neck,
right lower arm and my right foot. The pain
was indescribable and I said to my then-husband
sitting beside me. "It hurts too much to be
here." He then heard me take a deep guttural
breath, release it with a rattle, and my body
went perfectly still.

Instantly I was free from physical sensations, from physical realities. I was conscious of being **EVERYTHING** and **NOTHING** at the
same time. There were no boundaries, no lines
for demarcation or definition. I was in the
silkiest darkest space imaginable. It was a
well-lit velvety blackness. It was well lit in
the sense that my view, my vision, my awareness, was infinite and clear while I was safely
and securely embraced by love. It was light
and dark equally and easily.

I felt the presence of all things before,
during and after the existence I had known as
Mary in the crunched car. I was one with
everything while maintaining completely my
personal unique essence. Although my awareness
said this was what we call "death" my awareness
also knew that we don't really die, we only
change forms infinitely. The most common and

greatest human fear of death is that we end, that we lose ourselves. But now it was totally known to me, known throughout my wholeness, that it is impossible to end. This was both reassuring and a rude awakening. I was relieved to feel my infiniteness, but the reality that I couldn't run away from myself was just as true. This truth was a comfortable truth because it was also clear to me that I was totally one with this "higher power" this "God," this Love," this "Isness," this "Tao," this "Allah," or this "Almighty Creative Power." The term used to describe it is irrelevant. Only the awareness of the essence seems important to remember. The oneness of the Love/Almighty Creative Power is comfort. Love, the Almighty Creator, empowers everything. Love is all that is necessary to learn. Our ultimate goal is to consistently remember our oneness with Love. The Creator, Love, is the verb, the noun, the adjective, and the adverb, of, in and through all things visible and invisible. Love is the Almighty Creator infinitely.

I felt totally loved and accepted without criteria. I felt all knowing infinitely and simply. I knew that whatever I wished to know or understand was already within me, and simply by wondering about it I could access the answers.

I exercised what was obviously my choice to return to **this** reality (or "illusion"). And as we focus on a specific reality, we are also choosing to forget (vaguely) the rest of the universe. It's like believing we can't read every book in the library at the same time. So, we choose one book, one life, at a time while all the others exist simultaneously. Because we believe in boundaries, definitions, descriptions, images, feelings and thoughts as specific and individual increments, we then accept the illusion that we are as separate from the whole when, in truth, there are no bound-

13

aries, definitions. In the infinite all-space/non-space, all is one and one is all superimposed upon itself. It is only if we accept the perception of being separate from the Almighty Creator that we are able to create things that can be described.

Writing a description of the true awareness I experienced is the toughest, no, the most impossible thing to describe because in an effort to describe it, it becomes separate and dissected and it is then no longer truth. I can only offer you a **sense** of the real truth. But it is ... we are ... you are ... I am ... LOVE. It does sound cliche, but the truth is simply, LOVE.

So if I had written about my experience in real truth, my essay would have been one word: LOVE.

We don't have to die to remember. We don't have to experience the pain and suffering. It was my choice to return to life because I wanted to help create the most beautiful marriage possible on this earth. I wanted the marriage with my then-husband, but since there were two of us making the choices, and I still had a lot of changes to make with the woman in the mirror, it didn't work out with my first husband. I say "first husband" since I will courageously and consciously try again. I've realized that what we long for resides inside us. I knew this in my head for years, and I have been very successful as an educator and therapist helping others realize their inner strength and peace; however, being as stubborn as anyone born under a Taurus rising and a Taurus moon can be, it is taking more time than I like getting that information from my head and heart to my behavior. It gets easier and easier to be fully honest with myself and everyone I interact with, and with the near total healing of extensive physical injuries, I'm LEARNING to let go of pain and accept joy, peace and LOVE as my new companions. Learning ... In our physical realities we perceive separateness which suggests the opposite of the true infinite connectedness. Also, in this physical reality we misbelieve. So it is necessary to transfer, or learn, the truth I found to the experiences shared in living.

Living is a magnificent piece of art, a masterpiece of love in action. Through introspection we can effortlessly remember that LOVE is our natural state of being. I often remember the infinite love source from which I am created by using self-hypnosis, play, laughter, prayer and meditation. I'm still human, growing all the time; but I visit "Home-Love" often and it glorifies my life. I died to remember that I am born of the Almighty Creative Power/Love. Now I'm retraining and reprogramming all the memory in all my physical cells to live the truth as consistently as humanly possible. I can often hear an inner voice guiding me, and I pray to act on it more consistently. The truth is that when I don't listen, I am acting out of fear. I will do my best to share with you how "remembering" helps me reshape my life into more consistent love.

RE-ENTRY

While my consciousness was outside of my physical being I was monitoring the physical situation to select a point of return when the pain my body was enduring would be bearable. This point in time was when the wreckage had been cut away, and they had put a board behind my back, a brace around my neck and they were about to lift me from the car. I was told later that it had taken them approximately forty-five minutes to cut me from the wreckage; but where my consciousness was, time didn't exist. During the time they were cutting me from the car, I was intermittently "touching in" with my body. I simply had the **THOUGHT** of reassuring my then-husband that I would be o.k. and that I would return. It seems as though my "thinking" of reassuring my husband was enough to have it happen in the physical world. Later when I questioned the paramedic who sat beside me in the car while I was being cut out, he told me I sat **perfectly** still, staring straight ahead, occasionally calling out to my husband and saying, "It's o.k." From where I was, I couldn't sense myself acting with the sound of a voice. My efforts were like thoughts and feelings that extended out into whatever, and wherever they were meant to be received.

After having the far reaching separation of my consciousness from my physical form, I was able, for a time, to move close to my physical form and away again. I felt control over when and how much I was able to be emersed with the physical form until I made a complete return while my body was in the ambulance. I remember knowing my body was lying on the stretcher with a paramedic squatting beside me looking for a vein to put an I.V. into. Knowing that it's hard to find a good vein in my arm, it seemed reasonable to wake up (or return to my body) so that I could tell him where to find a good vein. It was when my consciousness returned to my body that my vital signs began going haywire. Prior to that point, a paramedic on the scene said that my vital signs were good and normal while I was perfectly still and staring straight ahead.

I have some speculations regarding this information. Many severely injured or ill patients reportedly appear to rally. Vital signs are strong and within normal range just before dying. This suggests to me some generalized speculations. I see it as possible that while ones infinite soul/psyche is in the body, the fear and the soul's general reaction to the physical condition causes stressful physical readings. When the soul is released (or at least once removed) from the physical being, the physical being acts independently and functions on its own for a time before it ceases to continue. In some cases the soul returns before the body passes a point of no return. In other cases the body runs out of power, so to speak, before the soul can or wants to return. If this is a truth, then it is the soul that causes the obvious responses in the physical being. One could further speculate that it is possible that once the infinite soul/psyche gets out of the way of the body's direct channel with the Almighty Creator Love, that the body is for that time healed. When the body no longer is needed to house the soul it is allowed to return to the source

18

through death, disintegration, and evaporation so that the energy used to manifest the body can be transformed into new useful physical manifestations.

To continue my speculation - I would suggest it is possible that the soul had really left at the point when the body "appeared" to stabilize. The body appeared to stabilize because the soul was outside of the body and could not cause reactions to manifest through the body. When my infinite soul/psyche was outside of my physical body, my vital signs were fine. Then when my soul returned, I began reacting, with fear, to the pulsating gyrations my physical body was manifesting as a result of being broken and squeezed like in a vice while pinned in the crunched car.

It has appeared to me that since I returned from "outside" I have been using the information I gathered from the outside to reprogram, reframe the memory cells and beliefs within which I live. I find innumerable beliefs, and belief patterns, some of which I wish to reinforce and strengthen, and many I am continuing to improve, revamp, and in some cases erase completely. I am doing this as carefully as I am able, with the ultimate goal of synchronizing my physical being and actions with the truth of the infinite Almighty Creative Power - Love.

I am convinced that our soul/psyche has a definite affect on our physical condition. This appears to manifest through our thinking and feeling. What we think and feel is manifested in our experiences. These experiences show up in our dreams as well as in our awakened state. This truth is why visualization is so effective in changing a person's physical, emotional, and mental condition. Through visualization in a deeply relaxed state of mind, I have seen major changes occur for many clients. Not only have they been able to release past negative beliefs, but they have

19

release past negative beliefs, but they have also experienced immediate physical health improvements. Among the many examples includes a client who sent cancer into remission, and a client who ceased having heart attack symptoms. The heart patient who was in his late forties, overweight, and a heavy smoker and drinker, was even able to visualize cleaning out his arteries one hundred percent, and a following exam proved that he was successful. Our minds are powerful instruments. Our minds can co-create with the Almighty Creator = Love, and change our personal and universal worlds. I personally have eliminated allergies, hypothyroidism, and hypoglycemia from my own physical system. I used to be very allergic to cats. I now live with a cat, and I can bury my face in her fur without any negative physical reactions. It takes visualization with **belief** in the image to manifest a new reality. I still have a few areas requiring additional development in order to accomplish changes that will make my physical experience more enjoyable, and comfortable. Doing what it takes to make my personal and extended world healthier in every way is **loving** myself and the universe. It is letting the truth of "God," Love, shine through.

When I see the statement from a Christian Bible, "In the beginning was the Word, and the Word was God (period)," this means to me that in the beginning was LOVE, since God is love. All things follow from LOVE -**PERIOD.**

"Outside" in the ALL VELVETY BLACKNESS with an infinite BRILLIANT LIGHT I saw forever, in all directions. An analogy that helps me express what the blackness and light is for me is that I see the blackness as every color of liquid paint poured together into a pail. It is rich and luscious beyond description. Within the deep blackness is all things as one, blended together. However, while being a part of the black velvety liquid paint in the pail,

These are the very colors of a rainbow. With the light, I (and you) can bring the pail of black paints "to life" by separating them into time (sequence) and space by applying them one by one in various orders to blank canvases. This is what life is for. That is why life is called the "gift of life". It truly is a gift to be given all of the "everythings" and all of the "nothings" to place in whatever order and arrangement or combination ones **heart desires**. The nothingness is the space between things and colors that makes it possible for us to see each part individually. This individualization allows us to select and prefer each unique part, appreciating it with awe.

Speed and velocity seem to play parts in the separation/ individualization process of creating objects and experiences. But I am not a physicist, so I will leave further explanation regarding these components to the proper specialized scientists. There are some excellent books written on this subject by experts such as Buckminster Fuller, Rupert Sheldrake and Richard Bohm.

Since I like to play with words, I noticed some years ago that the word L-I-V-E spelled backwards is E-V-I-L. Maybe it's when we resist our own power to co-create with the Almighty Creative Power - Love that we are behaving as evil. If this is truth, then I must admit with a chuckle that I am occasionally evil. The **devil** makes me do it. This is when I am live(ing) backwards, or with my back to the Light/Love/Almighty Creator.

Most importantly, I must emphasize here that every move, every thought, and every feeling we contribute to the universe has an effect, and is very meaningful. So, although I laugh at my foibles, I also take them seriously enough to continue to improve my performance and contribution to the whole. This sometimes feels like **real work**. But, I regularly remind myself to "play" it out consciously.

I will conclude this chapter/essay with a paragraph that came to me while in the middle of the Atlantic Ocean.

"The basic love energy forms into all things. Each form has different characteristics and capacities for expressing. The human form can communicate in the most complex ways. However, all energy (and all expressions of energy) communicate and interact with all other energy forms (i.e. its environment). Environment ultimately extends infinitely and enfolds into itself, and unto itself. This is the infinite universal love reality."

LIGHT ALONG THE WAY

May 1982

I sat extremely still and silent in the dim lit office staring at the oppressive wooden walls and heavy wooden furniture. The silence accented the sound of my pounding heart, piercing it like the sound of a dripping faucet in the middle of a sleepless night. My perspiring hands soaked the polished wooden arms of the chair I sat in. I wiped my hands on my J.C. Penney cotton skirt, then fumbled for a tissue from my purse to wipe the moisture from the rich wood. I looked out the narrow window to divert my attention from the tenseness I was feeling, only to see the wind jerking the leaves of a tree around in an abusive motion. Mesmerized by the action, I decided that the leaves and my heart had much in common.

I felt a rumbling sigh begin at my quivering knees, press up into my dry throat, and burst outward in a jolt. I remembered the earthquake I had experienced in Anchorage Alaska, and wondered if this was how the earth felt as pockets of gases rumbled and pushed their way up toward the surface, releasing thunderously, then settling down again through a series of quivers, shakes, and jolts.

A steadier, long and slow sigh rose from my groin with a volume that seemed magnified in the silence where I waited. I waited ... and I waited. I felt a numbness growing ever greater, until the opening of a creaking door startled me. A small framed doctor entered, carrying pages of paper he shuffled and read as he walked. Dr. Marku's dark olive skin common to his East-Indian heritage lent mystery to his serious posture.

As I watched him cross the room I wondered if this tiny man was weightless since I wasn't hearing his footsteps above the rattling of the papers.

"Hurry up and tell me, PLEASE!" I pleaded mentally. As I continued waiting, while watching the doctor - all in slow motion -I noticed my feelings. I wanted everything to be All Right, but at the same time it seemed that a crisis would be the natural course of events - very familiar, almost predictable. After all, I could handle anything! Hadn't I handled countless catastrophes in my thirty-five years, and always come out of them a "good" person? "I've seen this scene before, I know the part, I can play this role easily," I thought. "I'll listen closely, remember what is expected of me, and do it perfectly." I even began to see images of how everyone around me would respond. It was natural, human nature. But, before I can "start the action," as in a film, I need to know what the script is.

"Well?" I thought in my painful, "poor me" fashion. "Please tell me."

Dr. Marku walked slowly around his desk with his head bowed over the medical reports in his hands. He reached out with one hand to touch the arm of his overstuffed chair in order to guide himself into the seat, without looking up. As this dark little man behind a massive wood desk leaned his chair backwards he slowly raised his head to face me.

His voice snapped the fragile silence. "The last ultra sound shows the mass is much larger now, and the biopsy from the laparoscopy doesn't rule out malignancy. I think surgery would be the best solution; however, you do

24

have other options, and I will go over all of
that with you."

I was stunned. His voice thundered in my
ears like an echo in the hall of an empty high
school. It had been like a game until now.
I'd been poked and probed with many and various
instruments for; pap smears, biopsies, and
abdominal and vaginal examinations. I remembered the unending personal questions with a
renewed exhaustion. That was all behind me.
I felt frightened ... frightened and anticipa-
tory.

Anger began building, as I recalled how
so many doctors had told me that the chronic
and increasingly excruciating pain I had en-
dured for years, "was just something I'd have
to live with." I felt my facial muscles
tighten and twitch as multitudes of feelings
began to surface. My jaw stiffened, as I
remembered one doctor look down his nose at me
and say, with disinterest, "All women have female pain."

I felt disgust for macho male doctors who
appeared to think they were THE ONE AND ONLY,
ALL POWERFUL, GOD HIMSELF. To think I had
almost bought into their game of female weak-
ness vs. male power. My rage built into a roar
as I spoke my thoughts out loud, " I had almost
decided that I was just being overly sensitive
and temperamental. There really is a reason
for the pain! It's not that I had a low pain
tolerance level after all!" Suddenly, realizing that I had shouted in fury, I looked for
Dr. Marku's reaction.

He sat there calmly, with what appeared
to be a sensitive look on his face. I studied
the doctor's gentle face as thoughts continued
to flood my mind. Games of Life. What is life
after all? What is power and submission? My
father died of a malignant brain tumor when I
was fifteen; he was only forty-nine. Am I
going to die at thirty-five? I literally shook
my head, as if I could shake those frightening

25

from my mind. I released myself from a nauseous daze just in time to hear the doctor say, "You have three options."

Dr. Marku spoke slowly and clearly, "You can tell me that you don't want surgery, and I can try to treat you with medications. You can tell me to do the surgery, removing only the uterus, not the ovaries or tubes. We would use medications to try to clear up the rest; or you could decide to have me remove it all (uterus, tubes, and both ovaries) and thus be very certain that we get everything dangerous."

I heard him, yet I didn't. I asked question after question, until I felt I understood what my options were. I grew more and more comfortable with the doctor as he patiently drew pictures of the uterus, tubes, and ovaries. He showed me where the huge mass had already grown large enough to envelope my left ovary and tube, and surrounded my uterus. He explained how it could possibly be effecting my right tube and ovary.

I was impressed with this wonderful man who was willing to take the time to make certain that I had all the information I needed to make an educated choice regarding my own medical treatment. The next step was mine.

I headed for my car and the drive home, bursting with thoughts and feelings. I felt confused and anxious, a coming and going numbness, frightened yet determined, and alone in my own little world within a massive world.

As I began driving, I was vaguely aware of the steering wheel I clenched with my dripping palm and fingers. The street noise barely helped me drive safely. I felt detached from my physical senses. Even the mellow music that had always been so soothing to me seemed somewhat like a voice through an overseas telephone line.

I thought about life and what it meant. What meaning did my life have? What was my life all about? I thought about moments of love and joy in the middle of oceans of pain and fear. I looked inward for the **stuff** that would pull me through this critical time. Where was the **stuff** that had been there in other times of need? **What** was this stuff? Then, I saw the traffic light as I passed through an intersection, and the light seemed to soothe me. Light had always been a comfort to me. I remembered being ten or twelve years old and the winter sunlight would shine through the window and warm my surface and my soul as I curled up on the sofa like a lazy kitten. Light is soothing, I thought. I felt myself drift into a reverie. LIGHT.

. . .

This earlier critical experience, six years prior to the death-experience had a dramatic effect on the course of my life, similar to the death-experience of February 9, 1988. The critical surgery of August of 1982 corrected the problem and improved my health ten-fold. My life in general changed dramatically in multitudes of ways. Since the summer of 1982, I have made a firm commitment to cleanse my life and make it happy ... make it true ... make it real ... make it LOVELY. I have been releasing anger, as well as many other emotions, that were getting in the way of happiness.

My healing journey has not been entirely smooth, nor entirely chaotic. There have been times of "riding the rapids" as well as times smelling the sweetness of the fruits of my labor. Although I appreciate the gentle serenity of the cool ponds in the heat of the summer, I also completely appreciate the rocks and bumps in the river. After all, a stream without rocks would have no song.

There have been several transitional phases being processed in my life simultaneously. I share with you on these pages those experiences that at this point in time I am "faithful" enough to disclose. My sister recently said to me that she thought I had a great deal of courage. Her remark somewhat surprised me because I had not thought of myself as courageous. I offered no reply, but my thoughts dwelled on it for days. Then I confidently called her back to say, "Dee, I've been thinking about what you said. It has been on my mind because I haven't seen myself as courageous. But after a lot of thought, I wanted to tell you that what I think you are seeing as courage is not so much courage, as it is FAITH."

We had a delightful conversation, sharing in a way we hadn't for years, if ever. I am so glad I took the time to discuss with Dee how I have been focusing on trying to consistently remember that LOVE is in charge of my life, and therefore relax. I am still working on breaking old bad habits of acting with fear. The progress is noticeable, and definitely worth the effort.

In my transitions I included a spell of arrogance and social climbing, as well as a course in suicidal thoughts and depression. I have undertaken a major house cleaning commitment. In the recesses of my darkest closets and drawers, I have found treasures as well as rotten fermented garbage. Sometimes, the cleaning of the day was easy and refreshing; while other times it was enough to make an iron stomach convulse. It is all worth it because my life is becoming more spacious and brilliant, filled with love and laughter, and with a fantastic view of the LIGHT. My days of enLIGHTenment are more and more often, and the following poem was written on such a day.

DUCK'S EYES

I looked into a duck's eyes today.
Eye to eye: closely
        shared souls, and a cracker, I
            touched his essence gently.

I felt the sounds of a water lily
        blooming.
I heard a child sleeping in the shade
        of a tree.
I tasted the rolling hills and farms
        as I traveled through them.

I merged with the foliage as
        it brushed my shoulder,
            inhaling its essence.

The tree's bark blended with my spine.
The sun warmed my surface, and
        my depth.
I integrated with God's world, and
        felt the power of love.
Nature, the messiah of letting go,
        letting grow.

Nature taught me to love embodied souls the
        same as nature:
            letting go,
                letting grow.

The gentle rhythm of universal tides
        rides with me today.

Today is all I have, today.

Being now.
        Loving and letting loving be,
            Now.

PIN-HOLE PICTURES

Light Creations

When I was in second grade I found a favorite way to pass the time in school when I had completed assignments and was waiting quietly and patiently for the teacher to give us another assignment. I would take a straight pin and a piece of paper and poke holes in the paper to create a picture in the paper. Then I would hold the paper up to the light in the window so that the light would shine through the holes and make my picture "come to life." I loved doing this. It felt like a memory of warmth and love. I felt wonderful as I would gaze at the sparkles of light forming the picture.

I believe it's possible that children maintain a connectedness to the "outside" (wholeness of our universe) and gradually focus more and more on the physical world in which they live as they grow into adulthood. If this is true, then it stands to reason that I was "remembering" in much the same way when I was at an even younger age of two. At two years old I saw everything in our family garden as vibrating sparkles of light. The vegetables were like a collection of light particles of various colors and vibrational speeds acting as a group to "suggest" the form of the vegetable. The recollection of the visions at the age of two returned to me through self and guided hypnosis (simple guided imagery) under professional care.

The two situations I have just referred to are offered here as a preface to a description of what things looked like to me for a time after my psyche (infinite consciousness) returned to my body after the accident of February 9, 1988. Everything was vivid, vibrating, effervescent, and sparkling. For example, when I was released from the hospital, the ambulance attendant carried me into my house and sat me on the hospital bed that had been positioned, at my request, in front of the patio door. I looked out the window at the snow-laden pine trees and I felt aglow with the "light show." I saw sparkling green spruce needles and glistening snow "dancing" before my eyes. It was so awesome I called out with overwhelming tears of joy and love and asked my family to look at God/Love expressing itself in the trees and snow.

If you refer to the books in print by Drs. Moody and Morse, which contain extensive collections of case studies of persons having NDEs (near-death-experiences), you will find that it is common for those who have had NDEs to see things as I did for some time after returning.

What meaning does this have?

For me it has meaning regarding a new understanding of time and reality. I see it as an infinite all encompassing light, which by way of separation, suggests an image. The "light" **appears** to be a form, a shape, an idea, or an image for us to respond to, and interact with. The paper created spaces between the light shining through the pin-holes suggesting an image. Time and space are similar to a kaleidoscope. Imagine an infinite kaleidoscope in which there are uncountable particles which take on different colors, visibility, and form as we turn it around. Actually, we don't turn

32

it around, instead we change our personal perspective by putting ourself in various positions in relation to the infinite particles. This causes us to perceive particular appearances. Each **appearance** is like a gift of LIFE. Each perspective creates for us the appearance of a specific collection of particles in a certain order with certain light reflections. We then react to these presentations with our feelings and thoughts causing a reality for ourself and all particles involved (which can include other souls-psyches). These are the "illusions" that Richard Bach writes about in his book entitled ILLUSIONS. Life is an expression of LOVE. It is an expression of the LOVE LIGHT.

It is this kaleidoscope of life, this continuous repositioning of ourself in relation to the infinite and constant existence of the Almighty Creative Love Energy = LIGHT that results in the appearance of specific life experiences.

You see, life is not the opposite of death. Life has no opposite. Life is infinite. Death is simply being in the infinite and constant, forever present, LOVE ENERGY without the spaces and reflections. Death is being in the pail of paint (all the luscious colors poured together) with all the colors and quality of the Almighty Creator/Love blended together. Life is the positioning of oneself to enable visions and experiences via LIGHT, for the purpose of adoring the unlimited parts of the whole, individually.

There is an all encompassing Almighty Creator - LOVE LIGHT, from which we are, by which we see, through which we feel, with which we do, as which we experience the Beyond, and yet including, time and space.

Within this truth we are co-creators with the Almighty Creator-LOVE. With the ultimate truth of LOVE being the victor in the end, even if we spend life-times imagining separation.

Ultimately we are the LOVE. We are the LIGHT. We are one with our Almighty Creator-LOVE.

SPIRITUAL

Spiritual. This term first needs to be defined as it is being used in this text, and as I now define it based on my death/love experience. Spiritual is being of spirit. Spirit is of the Almighty Creative energy. Spirit is the essence from which we and everything else comes into being. Spirit is the emotion, or energy-in-motion. Spirit is emotion, or the Almighty Creator in motion through our piece of the whole. When something is said to be spiritual, it is a recognizable example of emotion, the Almighty Creator/Love in action.

An obvious example of being spiritual is when one is in meditation or prayer and consciously focusing on the Almighty Creator/Love. However, there are infinite and various examples of being spiritual. One comes to mind from a recent conversation I had with my friend Jim who is a competitive runner. As I listened to Jim speak of his dearly loved running, I could see his spirit rise and expand in its visibility. He was obviously letting the Almighty Creator/Love energy flow forth as he spoke of the activity that aided him in being fully in synchronization with the Almighty Creative Love Power. I told him that the best experience I had ever had regarding running was as a spectator. It was when I was visiting Chester, England, standing on a sidewalk overpass that crossed over a street connecting to the two buildings on either side of the street.

As I stood there looking down at the narrow brick street, I watched a mass of runners fill the street wall to wall moving toward me, under me, and past me. I felt an overwhelming feeling of devotion, commitment, and intense passion and love for their activity well up from the runners in the street and fill my being. As I described this to my friend, he got extremely excited and said, "Yes, you felt them being in the **spirit** of the run." This was truly a spiritual experience.

Let me expand on how I can refer to a physical activity as a spiritual experience. It isn't because it is a physical activity that it is spiritual. It is because the attitude and feeling in the activity is spiritual. Being aware of the essence in which it is happening is spiritual, which is equal in quality to the Love/Almighty Creative Power. It is actually the Almighty Creative Power that is empowering the activity/experience/object-/persons in the first place. Many different athletes experience spiritual sensations while participating in the athletic activity of their choice. It is not because they have chosen the "right" activity, but because of the way they are experiencing (feeling) it, they are aware of the Love, the Source, and the Power that creates the experience in the first place.

The approach to anything, athletic or otherwise, is the way spiritual experiences are realized. There have been occasions of intense spirituality when I have been observing a tiny leaf. As I focused on its creative beauty I felt a very moving spiritual flow of energy throughout my being. I could actually sense and vicariously experience what it might be like to be a leaf with its veins and textures and how it interacts with its environment. Whatever the experience, it is a matter of breathing into the activity, experience, or object and feeling a sense of its essence with love and appreciation, even with awe of its reality. When we approach life with an attitude which allows us to be aware of the power from which everything comes, we are then **REALIZING** the spirit of it, the love of it. The one statement that had the most impact on me in my childhood Christian upbringing was that "God is Love." I believe that. But, I also now see that the term God is a synonym for other words that label the Almighty Creative Power/Love, and I no longer limit my spiritual perspective to any one man-made doctrine that works toward tying us all-together again (religion). It appears that all religions have the same ideal purpose, even though at times human egos occasionally get off balance and believe that they must be special to be accepted by the Almighty Power. In truth, being special is impossible because each and every particle in the infiniteness is already as great as it can be from the perspective of the Almighty Creative Power/LOVE. It is a silly game that is played when we try to be more than the already infinite **MOST**. I often catch myself acting on socially conditioned beliefs that suggest I must prove to be special in order to be accepted or respected. When I remember to let go of these human social beliefs, I remember that since I am one with the Almighty Creative Power (as was shown to me when I died) I need prove nothing. I am already infinitely loved, accepted and respected "as is." When we accept that we are already perfect in the eyes of the Almighty Creative Power we let go of actions born of our fear of rejection. Acting on love instead of fear creates a world for all in which the truth of Love is more and more visible and felt by all.

Applying the word spiritual to relationships is the same truth as with activities, experiences, and objects. When we have a spiritual relationship we are relating with an attitude of love, respect, and even awe of the other person or persons involved.

37

Jim's running is something he **truly** loves. He was experiencing love of himself as he was partaking of the experience in which he allowed the love energy to flow through him. We do this through a variety of means, thanks to the Almighty Creator/Love. An example is the way new lovers look at each other as if the simple sight of the loved one will make them melt. Their eyes are dreamy, they can't seem to keep from touching one another, and they seem so focused upon one another that they appear somewhat disoriented to their surroundings. Another example is when a new mother feels the rush, the exhilaration, of having their newborn child announced as being healthy, especially the breathtaking sensation that comes when the new life, the new baby, is laid upon the mother's abdomen. "So this is the miracle that has been growing inside me all these months!", a new mother might say.

Jim had previously professed to me that for years he had been an agnostic, but that now he wasn't sure where he stood. Later in our conversation about running, he said that he could possibly say that running was his religion. I see this as an accurate and beautiful truth for Jim. It doesn't mean that he is putting running before the Almighty Creator, Love, but that through running he is experiencing the Almighty Creator/Love. To call running a religion seems very appropriate to me since the epistemology of the word religion is that it means - to tie together again. For Jim, running has tied him together again with the Almighty Creator/Love Power.

When I first learned, in a World Religions class in college, that the word religion means "to tie together again," the thought that followed for me was that religion's purpose is to do away with itself. After all, if religion can completely tie us together again with the Almighty Creator then religion would no longer be necessary. This seems rather beautiful to me. It's quite like the caterpillar dying to set the butterfly free to soar.

To conclude on what spiritual is to me, I would simply like to say that spirit is love. Therefore, being spiritual is being loving with all things of the universe since all things are borne from the Almighty Creative Power/Love itself.

I closed my eyes, relaxed and remembered ...

AUGUST 1949

The soft moist earth tickled my toes as it oozed between them. I felt my two year old body giggle as I laughed. The smooth touch of the silk on the corn cobs was gentle, and soft. As I bent to see more closely beneath the leaves of the cucumber plants I noticed the skin on my thighs press against the skin on my calves. I was delighted with the sensations.

Clear blonde hair fell into my eyes creating a lovely veil, and another perspective of my environment. I felt thoroughly pleased with myself for choosing to inhabit my spirit in this tiny human body. At two years old, I could still remember having been purely spirit and yet I was enjoying learning to operate in a physical human form.

My thoughts flowed serenely, "I love this garden spot. I treasure the many luscious moments here in precious solitude and wonderment. I enjoy my garden fully with my senses while my mother and older sister labor in the kitchen preparing food for supper, as well as food for the winter to come. They're canning vegetables and fruits. I like looking into the glass jars full of nourishment that appears swelled and glossy."

My father tended the fields and the cows while I spent precious moments in the garden tantalizing my senses. I was enjoying the twinkling lights that created the imaginary garden forms. The vegetables were not only a beautiful sight, but the smell, touch, taste, and the textures made me tingle. My physical senses were magnified by a childlike awareness of a sixth sense. This sixth sense told me my garden was only a little piece of infinity. My sixth sense told me that this was one single expression of the Almighty Creator/Love.

The hot August afternoon was especially pleasant in my garden where the tall corn shaded my small body with a welcome coolness. As I stood in the cool shade of the corn I saw a tall, dark, thin man approaching. "Maybe he wants to enjoy its pleasures as I do. It would be nice to have a playmate.", were my easy thoughts.

"I have seen this man before, helping my father plow the fields, and milk the cows. My family welcomes him when he is here. He must be a friend." I thought comfortably.

"Come play with me." I spouted excitedly to the man as I skipped between the rows of vegetables.

He broke into a wide toothy grin.

"You like it here in the garden, don't you?" he asked.

"Un huh!" I bounced back.

He shifted his eyes to the side, wetted his lips, and asked, "Do you like to play in the barn?"

"Can't go there. I'm too small. Daddy says to stay outdoors."

"I'll take care of you in the barn." he returned.

I paused to think. "This man is a friend to Mommy and Daddy. Daddy lets him be in the barn. He helps Daddy there. If he helps me there, then I guess I can go there and have a big person take care of me. Besides, I saw the bigger kids laugh, run, play, and swing on ropes in the barn. They were having lots of fun there in the hayloft too. I wonder what is so much fun in the hayloft?"

"Umm Hmm. I want to play in the barn." I chirped.

42

The friendly tall thin man led the way into the barn that sat on a gentle hill, and smelled of such wondrous smells. It was cooler in the barn, in the shade it created. And there was a soft refreshing breeze that flowed from one end to the other through the partially open doors.

The barn was very quiet this afternoon. The cows were out to pasture, and the only sounds I heard were the tiny feet of chickens rustling about in the straw in the corner stall.

"I like the smells and stuff in the barn. But I'm not 'spose to be here" I said.

Just as I started to turn and walk out, I heard the man say, "I'll carry you up to the hayloft if you want."

"Oooo, the hayloft. Really?"

"Sure, here I'll put you on my shoulders. Hang on tight while I climb the ladder." he told me.

I felt as if I were floating in mid air as he picked me up with his very strong arms. It happened so quickly that it was as if the ground had disappeared from beneath my feet. As I sat high on his shoulders, I held on so tight with my legs that it pinched my inner thighs. I didn't want to fall. And the hayloft looked so high! ... and so dark!

As he stepped onto the hayloft floor, he reached up and took me from his shoulders and placed me on a bale of hay. The hay was scratchy on the soles of my bare feet. It had a sweet smell of sunshine mixed with a pungent wet earthy smell at the same time.

I suddenly felt frightened. Something inside me said "Beware," and instantly my physical senses seemed to shut down. I no longer noticed the scratchy hay or smelled anything. My sense of FEAR grew stronger and overpowered all other sensations. The man I thought was a friend, put his big rough hands on either side of my head and held it so tightly that my ears hurt.

"Ouch!" I cried.

"Now hold still!" he said fiercely.

I gasped as he took a long hard meaty part of his body from inside his trousers and pushed it into my mouth.

I gagged, choked, and struggled for air. The hardness he pressed against the back of my throat was painful, and I couldn't catch my breath.

I started swinging my arms in panic. I broke away and fell backwards off the bale of hay, and onto the loosely constructed wood floor of the hayloft. I rolled away, wanting to escape. "CRACK! SNAP!" The slat of wood I was on gave way. I fell through the floor screaming as I landed in the straw-filled concrete gutter below.

My body both ached and was numb at the same time. I panted for air, and my arms and legs screamed with pain. Then everything went dark ... When I awoke I barely felt my mother's hands pick me up and fold me into her breasts, and brush my hair away from my face.

"How on earth did you get in that hayloft? You know you aren't supposed to be in the barn! Let's look at you. I guess you're ok, except for a few scrapes and bruises." were my mother's words. "Come sit in the kitchen with me while I finish kneading the bread. It has to get into the oven before supper."

My sobs were beginning to soften now. But my fear, and confusion were mounting to a peak. I felt numb and swollen from the inside out. Hot tears ran down my cheeks, and my head throbbed with pain. My throat ached so much, that my breath passing in and out felt like a rake.

I could hear impatience and weariness in my mother's tired voice as she said, "For heaven's sake hush now. You'll be alright."

"I guess it's my fault." I thought

silently to myself. "I was bad for going into the barn with the man. It's my fault." I thought. "I shoulda known better."

I wobbled over to the tall painted wood-framed kitchen window. The sill was low enough for me to lean on. I loved this window with the uneven paint layers that I stroked with my tiny tender fingers. I especially loved the shear curtains trimmed with lace. The lace had a trillion holes I could look through. It created a collection of light sparkles as the sun shone through the openings of the lace.

The window hadn't changed. The curtains were the same as ever. And the lacy holes I had loved were still there. But I felt different now. These familiar items brought me some comfort, but it wasn't quite the same. I saw my garden from the window, and my stomach churned. I had seen my garden world as a wondrous play-land for loving with my senses. But, it appeared more solid now. I didn't quite see the twinkling lights I used to see. Other things looked different now also. I noticed that not everyone felt as I did. And, I decided that men were something to be frightened of.

I could smell bread baking, and hear my mother behind me scurrying about the kitchen putting supper on the big, white enamel, metal table. I used to like playing under the table as if it were my own little house. But what used to feel like a comfortable shady place was now frightening dark shadows.

Dad came in with a squeak from the back-door and the shuffle of his boots upon the kitchen linoleum. I could smell the earth on his hands as he went to the sink to wash them. I turned from my window to see him, and for a moment gasped at the image of this tall strong man. Then my eyes focused more clearly, and I knew this was my father, a gentle man. A man who had never hurt me. Actually, he hardly ever touched me, or spoke to me.

45

I ran to Dad's side and wrapped myself around his denim leg. My sense of touch seemed restored as I stroked the weave of his bib overalls.

"Alright. Alright. Let go of me now so I can get to supper. I still have the cows to bring to the barn, and the milking to do before dark."

I looked for a moment of reassurance, but was quickly sent back to my own little world of sights, sounds, smells, tastes, textures, and an inner awareness that I didn't know how to express.

My inner awareness told me that I was like the air I breathed - fresh, pure, and just as important. My inner awareness was still in touch with a deep love that was difficult to express among the busyness of the people in this world. It was the luscious nature, and the lacy light reflections on the glass window panes that helped me remember the powerful light of love beyond the new cloud of pain my senses had experienced.

...

I sighed, relaxed and remembered more ...

1952

I played in the boxes that my mother was packing. I'd been told we were moving south to the city. Moving to the city where Dad could get work. I didn't really understand everything they told me. I was only 5 years old. All I new was that we were leaving the farm. The farm. A place that had been my whole world until now. What and where would I feel, sense, and express next? I was a little frightened, and at the same time I wanted to know what the city had to offer.

"Now you kids go and play. I have work to do." Mom shouted at me and my brother.

46

My brother was two years older than me, and an adventuresome boy. Usually he was off on great explorations with my father. He seemed important in my eyes because he got to do things with Dad. He seemed important and powerful. He wasn't usually in the house much, but, today a rainstorm kept him inside with me. I had a playmate, something I didn't often have.

Jimmy, my brother, went into Mom's and Dad's room with me, just off the kitchen where Mom was packing things from the cupboards. I started bouncing on the bed, but stopped when I saw Jimmy with something that looked like the matches Mom used to start the stove.

"What have you got there?" I asked excitedly.

"Matches. An **don't** you tell Mom either, or I'll **get** you for it."

"Can I see?" I asked.

"We can't let anyone know we have them. Let's hide under the bed." Jimmy suggested.

We crawled under the bed, and Jimmy lit a wooden stick match by striking it on his jeans. Instantly there was light. I stared into the flame, and felt a sense of peace I remembered feeling, somewhere, sometime before. The flame was warm, and bright. I remembered how warm, bright, light had seemed like love to me somewhere, sometime in the past.

I liked the match game we played under the bed. Jimmy even let me strike one, and watch the flame spout from the end of the stick. First it was blue, then a bluish-red color, and it finally settled into a bright golden light. I held the flame close to my face so that I could feel enveloped by its power. Then I smelled a pungent smell and saw smoke.

"Oh no!" I screamed. "My hair is on fire!"

The once beautiful experience turned instantly into panic. I scurried from beneath the bed and ran into the kitchen so Mom could save me from becoming one big flame from head to toe.

"OH MY!: mother gasped as she grabbed me, and put my head under the kitchen faucet.

"Sizzle, hiss." went the water as it put out the fire in my hair.

"Where did you kids get those matches?" Mom demanded. Neither of us said a word.

I wanted comfort and reassurance. But, the expression on Mom's face, and the tone in her voice, only offered anger, criticism, and rejection.

"I guess I'm bad." I thought. "I'm bad, and that's probably why I have bad painful things happen to me." I decided.

"Maybe things will be better in the city. Maybe I'll feel better there," I wondered and hoped.

The next morning we all crowded into the family car, all six of us. I sat on my oldest sister's lap and leaned against the window as the ride to the city stretched on and on. I gazed at the sun reflecting on the chrome around the window. The longer I stared, the more peaceful I felt. I found myself thinking, feeling, and remembering many things.

I remembered my garden and the crunch of the pickles Mom made from the baby-sized cucumbers. I enjoyed that memory, until I remembered that my older sisters got to help Mom make things in the kitchen, and they always told me "Go play. You're in the way."

I remembered my garden and how much fun it was to go bare-foot in the soil after a rain. I remembered the worms enjoying the soil as much as I did. But as I thought of the garden, and the shade of the corn stalks in August, I felt my stomach quiver, and my shallow breathing become irregular. Then I thought of the shade in the barn, and the fear in the darkness of the hayloft. I remembered the man - I remembered the PAIN. I remembered feeling

the sense of rejection from my parents when
they had expressed anger at me for being in the
barn. The memory of my garden had been transformed from a fun place to a terrible place.
My lips began to tremble. I pressed them hard
together and my mouth was firm and tight as I
felt rage fill me up. Then I sucked in a deep
breath of air, letting it out with a shaky
sigh. Tears swelled in my eyes. I didn't like
this memory at all - I won't remember it anymore I decided.

"The man ... men," I wondered, "are men
something to fear? All men?"

"Oh not Dad. Dad would never hurt me. No
not Dad. Everyone says Dad is a saint." As I
thought these thoughts I noticed a growing
uncertainty and confusion that was new and
uncomfortable. I didn't know how to sort it
out. So I pushed it deep inside, hoping it
would go away.

As I continued remembering, I was trying
to figure out the meaning of it all, as best I
could with my young mind. I figured, I loved
everything, but sometimes things happened to
me, or I did things, and people would reject me
or be angry at me. "I guess I should be more
careful to be **good**. ... whatever that means.
I will watch very closely, and learn the **rules**
of this game, because I like it when people
show me affection, and love me."

I continued to stare at the light reflecting off the chrome around the car window.
It now reminded me of the bright warmth I had
felt from the light in the flame of the match
and the light that glistened on the rain pud-
dles after a cooling rain on a hot summer day.
The light dancing on the car chrome also reminded me of another light. A light that was
indescribable. As I watched the sunlight dance
back and forth on the car's chrome I felt as if
it were actually me, and I was the warm light.
I was the light. This thought was comforting,
and I gently eased into a soothing half sleep,

49

safe, and secure, and feeling loved. It was a love I didn't know how to describe, but I was very glad I could still remember it, and feel it when I needed it.

I drifted off into a nap thinking, "Maybe there will be lots of light in the city, lots of love ...

I remembered these things as I relaxed, and after a brief silence, I heard my own voice from a cassette player suggest that I look at my experiences from the outside looking on. "See the events as if you are a third person," my voice on the cassette suggested. "What does Mary need? the voice asked. The voice was briefly silent while I did as asked with my inner child. After a pause I heard, "Embrace her now ... Tell her she is loved from the inside out, and erase the pain." the voice said.

In my mind's eye and fullness of my heart I loved and embraced my little self with for-giveness ... giving forth to me so much love that it oozed from my pores and overflowed into the environment. I remembered the memory of being a light among lights. I felt peace and security, as well as a sense of being saturated with love. Old, stale, inappropriate misper-ceptions and judgments melted away.

The voice on the tape asked me to look at everyone involved in the experiences. I thought of the man in the barn. I thought of the lack of love and attention from my busy, overworked parents, and the tears flowed. I asked the little inner child, from the third person perspective, what she needed. And I heard the little girl in me say, "Just love me. Just love me." I cried a softer cry now. I cried a healing cry as I imagined in my mind and heart embracing my little child self ten-derly. I was finding a peace within as I cuddled my little self, and stroked my little face and hair. There no longer was any room for finding fault or blame. There was no more guilt. There was simply love. Enfolded in love, I knew that everything else was simply an illusion.

As I looked at everyone involved I could clearly see they were acting out the social conditioning they had "learned." It was clear that there really was no one to blame. The scenario, the experience, was a manifestation of the "thinking" of the times, and the "thinking" of the individuals involved. It became obvious to me that guilt and blame would only perpetuate the illusions. These realizations helped me feel a fullness of PEACE.

Again I heard my own adult voice on the cassette player as it suggested that I make sure that everything had been cleansed, loved and accepted in the events remembered. After I completed this self-guided session of facing, embracing, and erasing, I knew that there were other buried memories to clean up. I was more anxious to face them now - knowing that greater and greater peace would follow. It was clear to me that the experience was not "who" I was. The experience was simply an experience, and not my identity. My personal value was not defined by the **experience**. So I went on ... I went on to reprogram my **thoughts**, and therefore my realities. I went on ... IN LIGHT, and IN LOVE.

Observations

Observation One

The original assault to my throat was not entered into my memory as a sexual experience. It was recorded in my memory as a painful physical experience. It wasn't until later when additional input throughout my life, regarding activities involving genitalia, molded the former experience into a collective memory that summed up an event to represent sexual abuse.

The <u>physical</u> experience did help me be more grounded into the physical world. An "intuitive" once suggested to me that I had still been teetering between the spirit world and the physical world until the intense physical impact helped get me here. I tend to agree with her. It's like the boy quoted in CLOSER TO THE LIGHT by Melvin Morse. When the boy was brought back with the paddles (shock treatment) in the emergency room he said, "Hey, you slammed me back into my body!" The physical assault to my throat by a penis might not have been the preferable way to get me grounded, but it was the experience that was immediately available. I am thankful for it.

Observation Two

There were multiple experiences when I
didn't feel loved. These experiences were
filtered through a learned system that was
based on believing in bad vs. good. I had
learned this accumulated system by way of
experience and observation. With a belief
system of good vs. bad in force, my young mind
interpreted multiple experiences as either good
or bad, right or wrong. I therefore regularly
looked for who or what to apply each term and
its meaning to. That resulted in my attaching
the "bad" label to myself. All children want
to see their parents as good. I was no different. I wanted to believe that my parents were
"good," and therefore capable of caring for my
many vulnerable needs. Even though at my
initial entry into this physical world of
boundaries and definition I had a temporary
memory of the LOVE LIGHT, as I moved into this
world of separation and definition, my interpretation of the experiences in the earlier
years of this life were affected not only by
the conditioning in this lifetime, but they
were also affected by experiences from other
times and places. The additional memories
would be memories coming from experiences in
other times and places - memories from other
lives. Even though we can remember the total
truth as being one with a LIGHT of LOVE infinitely, there are current experiences that
remind us of other physical experiences which
often cause us to react reflectively out of
learned **habit**. When we react out of learned
habit we are forgetting ourselves instead of
remembering our source: LOVE. I had begun this
life-time, knowing the truth of the LOVE LIGHT
.. that truth being that the LOVE LIGHT is our
Almighty Creator. I was still remembering the
truth, but only intermittently. While experiencing life I have noticed that there are other
parts and particles (including those operating

53

as humans) not consistently remembering the LOVE truth. I learned and accumulated input that was being entered into my subconscious computer - belief system. I was "conditioned" to operate within the system I live in. However, I am now looking very carefully at my behavior, thoughts, and feelings to consider whether my contributions are consistent with our LOVE Truth. I still have a long way to go, but I know I am on the path of the **simple** truth. LOVE is the beginning, the end, and everything in between. It has been written that "Nothing real can be threatened, and nothing unreal exists." This is a truth for me. Good and bad are unreal illusions, therefore they do not exist, except in our minds. Love is real and it cannot be threatened. Knowing, and remembering this brings me Peace and Serenity.

Observation Three

The adults in the scenarios described in this chapter had also "forgotten themselves." They had forgotten their true selves and learned to make a game of life. Systems (structures, rules, and guidelines for the games) have been gradually developing since the beginning of time. These systems are "BELIEF" systems. The systems operate by way of mutual, and collective agreement among all those participating in the reality that is being created by way of the beliefs and THOUGHTS. Each of us enter the society, and we learn the system unconsciously through thoughts, experiences, modeled behavior, and especially through attitudes transmitted even without observable activity. Systems have become extremely complex, and as we participate in them we perpetuate the system. We have forgotten that there are other options. We have become dependent upon what is familiar and accepted by the masses.

Observation Four

The following is written from a Christian base, but there are parallels in every religion or lifestyle. For those readers who are not Christians please insert the word that translates as "God" for you. With this in mind consider the following as possible truth:

THE LOVE PRINCIPLE

In the beginning there was God.
God = Love.
Therefore, in the beginning there was Love.
God is the Almighty Creator.
God = Love.
Therefore, Love is the Almighty Creator.
Love is All Creative.
LOVE CREATES ALL.
ALL IS LOVE.
Create is Action.
Therefore, CREATIONS are LOVE in ACTION.
ALL is LOVE.
Therefore, Life is love in action.
Love accepts ALL : every shade, every color, every combination.
Life is LOVE expressing itself infinitely.

If you can accept, or at least consider the above as true, then consider that somewhere along the line the creative power of love moved through a creative transition that has been described in the parable of the Garden of Eden. There are parables in other religions and lifestyles that are similar to the Christian "Garden of Eden" parable. Please consider the theme rather than getting caught up in the specific example. Consider it from the perspective that everything is LOVE.

A new explanation of "The Garden of Eden" :

Some part/particle/or whole of the Infinite Almighty Creator (God/Love) imagined or thought, and therefore "created," the **idea** of GOOD and BAD. The idea that opposites could exist was then born.

Within the new belief system in which opposites exist, participators began to categorize things and experiences into good and bad, right and wrong, black and white, etc.

Humor me as you consider that the Almighty Creator, which is LOVE, was transmitting continuous and infinite signals representing acceptance of **ALL** things, every atom in existence. Consider also that the signal also contains the following property: "as something is stated, thought, and felt - so it is." Beliefs, as thoughts, are powerful enough to create. This is parallel to how it was described in Genesis of the King James version of the Christian Bible of how God (LOVE) **said** "Let there be light, and there was light." LOVE/GOD was saying: desire it and so be it; think it, and it then exists. Let me elaborate on that thought with the following statement: If BLANK is what you desire, then BLANK is what you will experience. All the while this LOVE signal was being transmitted, it was being received and interpreted by humans into parables using the language of the time and place, and understood according to the vehicle receiving and interpreting the transmission.

So ... in the story about the Garden of Eden there is a line that goes something like this: "If you eat of the forbidden fruit, you will surely die."

Since, IN THE BEGINNING THERE IS UNITED INFINITE LOVE (GOD) AND ONLY LOVE, **nothing** else exists. Therefore, it is reasonable to say that the statement: "If you eat of the forbidden fruit, you will surely die." does **not** mean that there **is** bad and if you partake of bad then you will have your "light" put out.

It is also reasonable to say that the signal sent, and stated by a human mind as, "If you eat of the forbidden fruit, you will surely die." could mean - "If you embrace, consume (eat), accept, partake of (i.e. think) something like opposites as true for you, then there are such things as opposites like good, and bad **for you**. Believing in **forbidden** (bad) fruit (results) will bring you to experiencing that belief as true."

Take this another step further - Because you BELIEVE in "Forbiddeness," then death (an opposite) will be part of your illusionary reality along with good and bad. But death is only "real" by virtue of your BELIEF system. Even though the truth is that life has no opposite, LOVE allows us our silly creative mind games, including the one that suggests opposites. You see, LOVE loves us so much that it denies us NOTHING. So if we want to create good/bad, life/death, right/wrong etc, etc. then "so be it." But now that we know that we are "of," "from," "by," and "with" the same power as the total source: LOVE, the Almighty Creator, WHY NOT BEGIN LEARNING TO CREATE BELIEF SYSTEMS IN WHICH OUR THOUGHTS WILL BE JOYOUS, PEACEFUL, PRODUCTIVE, AND ESPECIALLY LOVING?!! We are like the acorns of the mighty Oak. God/Love is the mature, fully developed, all mighty oak. We are the acorns, the off-spring, the seedlings, the children of God/Love. We have everything in us necessary to be like our source, and produce results like the true nature of our source. SO LETS CHOOSE TO GROW UP INTO WONDROUS NATURALLY **LOVING** Oaks!

Because each and every living thing, including you and me, is of the MAIN SOURCE, every living thing has the same creative properties. That means you and I can create with our thoughts. Actually, we co-create with the collective original Almighty Creator which consistently contributes only LOVE in the interest of the WHOLE since to do otherwise is to undermine the self. Of course each one of us is **uniquely** an individual "part" of the whole; but EVERY part, particle, and atom of our essence is an equal contributor to the collective whole. Look at the word "whole" (w-holy) - isn't it likely that "whole" (w-holy) and "hole" (holy) originate from the same conception. So - the Father, Son, and Holy Spirit are: The Creator, the Created, and a Spiritual Whole as one. The thought and the manifestation are W-holy one in Spirit. Life is but a dream, an illusion, an expression of the one real unit: LOVE. Even though we **experience** cause and effect within the original LOVE system, it is still WHOLE in SPIRIT while no "real" separation occurs. No "real" experience, definition, or description occurs. An experience is an experience: a happening - not an identity. It's not who we are; it's what we're doing. The identity is the Wholeness of Spirit: LOVE. The Creative experience is an internal occurrence within the Whole of the Spirit, and with unlimited possibilities.

To know that our experiences are not our identity, and to know that we **learn** and **choose** systems, reminds us that we have the power to experience a different reality by learning and choosing, therefore creating new systems. There are unlimited types of systems expressed in our world. There are school systems, city systems, government systems, family systems, cultural systems, work systems, and social systems. We have an unlimited ability to collectively affect expressed systems infinitely. We have a responsibility (an ability to respond) with LOVE as our first and only truth.

RESPONSIBILITY

Responsibility is
    the ability to respond.

Choose a response
    within your abilities.

Accept it.

Expand your abilities:
    Expand your options.

Expand your responses.

Enjoy your
    RESPONSE ABILITY!

JOHN

I had paused a moment to scan my client's intake form ... John Bellamy, 28, B.A. Mathemathics, married, two children ...

The young man dressed in paint-stained denim pants and a carelessly worn cotton print shirt, sat contentedly relaxed in the supple, over-stuffed recliner. He casually looked around the decorative room of delicate blues and whites. The window shades were adjusted to yield only a subdued, and soothing mid-day light. After scanning the contents of the room, he settled for facing the flower arrangement of tranquil pink, blue, peach, yellow and leafy green. He seemed to be examining the imitation goldfinch that was part of the flower arrangement he was enjoying. His eyes softened and relaxed as he listened attentively to my voice.

"Focus your eyes on a tiny spot in front of you." I said. "Let that spot be **your** spot, John. And, know that there is no where else you need to be, except right here, right now, relaxing."

My voice drifted into a slow, soothing, soft tone. I suggested a sigh of relaxation by sighing with my own voice as I proceeded. "Now become aware of your breathing. And notice when you inhale, and exhale. Inhale completely, and easily, taking in clean, purifying oxygen. Pause. Exhale completely, and release all dis-**c-o-m-f-o-r-t**, all dis-**e-a-s-e**, and relax deeper, and deeper. Your eyes are getting heavier and heavier, and you may wish to close them, and see that it is more relaxing to let them be closed. Yes, that's right. Blinking your eyes, and becoming more and more relaxed. And now as your eyes are closed, you are deeply, and **very safely** relaxed. Letting go now. Relaxing."

I let him enjoy a few silent moments of the new level of relaxation he had reached. I enjoyed watching John's temperament change from the strained and distressed disposition he brought with him into my office this afternoon, to a serene relaxed posture. I recalled how he had tried to cover up his self- doubts, and his fears of responsibility for his new young family with a staunch and stubborn veneer. He had talked about having the right to do "his own thing" as he put it. He was searching for excuses to escape the wife and child who were looking to him for closeness, love and security. I noted the dramatic contrast between that young man, and the young man who was now before me, relaxing and at ease.

Then I continued with a voice that modeled progressive relaxation. "Now become aware of the surface beneath you, and how fully it supports you. Feel the texture of the fabric beneath your fingers, and relax deeper, and deeper. Feel the support of the surface beneath you, and let go, more and more; recognizing that your physical self is safe and secure, relax deeper and deeper. And, as you continue to relax more and more you will notice that you will remain mentally alert, but very, very relaxed, and as safe as you can possibly imagine. Know that you are in absolute control, and should you wish to awaken, for any reason, at any time, you will do so instantly within the millisecond it takes to have the wish. So relax, and know that as you let go more and more, you are safe and secure, physically, mentally, and emotionally." And, with a deep sigh I added simply, "Relax."

While allowing John to be thoroughly
aware of his relaxed, and safe state of being,
I let my own attention face the silence. But
it wasn't total silence, so I continued with a
hushed and trained voice, "And as you hear the
sound of my voice, or any other sounds, inside
or outside of our space, you will be more
relaxed and safe; noticing that your emotions
are also very, very relaxed, comfortable, and
safe. You are easily becoming very, very
relaxed. And as this process continues, as
easily as your breathing continues, in and out,
in and out, like the rhythm of the ocean's
tide, one breath after another, you will effortlessly find yourself, in your minds eye, in
a very safe place of your own making. It can
be anywhere, anything. It can be inside, or
outside, or a combination of these. It can be
someplace you have been to, a new creation of
your own, or a place you wish to be in that you
have dreamed of. You will find yourself there
easily and safely, as I count to 3. And on the
third count you will become aware of all that
your safe place has to offer." I went on with
a deliberate and soothing voice. "One - letting go of any remnants of dis-e-a-s-e, dis-c-
o-m-f-o-r-t, and letting yourself be in **your**
safe place. Two - almost completely there.
And **three, -** you are there, **now.** And tell me
about your safe place, knowing that as you
speak you will enhance your relaxation and the
loveliness of your safe place."

He moistened his lips, and awkwardly
manipulated the muscles of his mouth, as if
testing them to see if they would function in
this deeply relaxed state. He swallowed
gently, and began in a quiet slow tone, "It's
... I'm ... there's a tree. A very tall ...
big ... old ... and sturdy tree. Um ... maybe
an oak? Anyway, I like it. It gives me
strength. And the grass ... the grass is tall
and lush. Very soft where I'm sitting."

"Can you describe the colors you see?"
I questioned very gently so as not to disturb
the serenity of his experience.

"Green mostly." he said, "But, there's
different shades of green, some darker, and
some lighter."

"Is there anything else to see in your
safe place?" I quizzed.

"The sky is blue, and the sun is shining.
But, there's also some ... a few ... white
fluffy clouds in the sky."

"Do you feel safe with these things?"

"Yes." He answered with certainty.

"Let yourself feel this safe feeling
throughout your entire being as you notice if
there are any sounds, smells, or tastes in your
safe place."

"I hear the breeze rustling the leaves of
the tree. And there's a few crickets." He
allowed a little smile to show on his face as
he continued to notice the sounds and smells of
the safe place he was creating for himself. "I
hear a dog bark ... way over there." And he
waved his left arm as he spoke. "I smell the
moist earth, it's like just after a good rain."

As I listened and watched him describe,
and feel, his safe place, I noticed his posture
soften more and more, and his smile spread
throughout his whole being. After allowing him
time with his pleasure, and his peace, I
stepped in to enhance, and expand the benefits
of his safe place. "Being very aware of your
safe place with all your senses, and feeling
very, very, safe, let this safe feeling fill
you completely, every cell, every molecule,
every part and particle, every atom of your
essence with the feeling of safety, serenity,
and loveliness. Feel all of it in all of you,
now." I paused, and then asked, "Do you feel
it completely, now?"

"Yes." John answered firmly.

"Are you still aware of the sun above
you?"

"Yes."

"Can you feel the warmth of the sun warming the surface of your being?"

"Yes."

"Can you imagine that your own life force is like a light shining from your heart, from your soul, shining like a candle's light from the center of your being?"

"Um. Yes. I can."

I continued very slowly, as I paced myself with his breathing, his body posture, and my sense of his energy's mood. "Now let the light from the sun continue to warm you, and penetrate your physical being, until it merges with your own life's light. Then feel yourself completely surrounded, and saturated, with a protective light of love and life. Do you feel this, **now?**"

"Yes. I do." He said excitedly, yet softly.

"Your every cell, every molecule, every atom of your essence is safe, and saturated with a light of love and life. Let me know when you feel this totally, and know that it goes with you everywhere you go; and that you are ready to go on to look at things that can be cleansed, and healed, taking you to a more peaceful, and happier state of being today. Let me know when you are ready to move on, taking it all with you."

A brief silence passed before John answered, "I'm ready now."

"I will count again," I said, "and this time on the third count you will find yourself at the root of the problem, the dis-e-a-s-e, the dis-c-o-m-f-o-r-t that we have offered up today." As I said this, I knew that I didn't need to restate the anxiety we had discussed earlier, he knew within himself what our goal was; and I didn't want to limit his healing by my interpretation, or my personal word choices. So I continued, knowing that his subconscious mind knew what he would benefit the most from

65

at this given moment. "One - going back, back, back to the root of the dis-EASE, to the very beginning, taking the safety of the light of love and life with you. Two - almost there, and very aware of your safety, and the loveliness of the light that goes with you, feeling prepared to face, and heal, whatever will benefit you today. Almost there now, safely. And, **three!** - you are there, **now.** Tell me the first thought, feeling or image that comes to you no matter how simple it seems."

The pause seemed long, and I watched the look of confusion spread across his face. His mouth twisted in puzzlement. Then he spoke. "I don't understand."

"What don't you understand?" I questioned, in a sensitive yet commanding voice in order to draw into words what was going on in his mind.

"Well, it my friend's face. My old friend." And as he spoke his facial muscles twisted up as he was trying to hold back the anguish and tears that suddenly filled him. "My friend!" he nearly screamed with a voice full of many emotions. "And he's dead!" he concluded as the tears stained his cheeks and ran down his throat and onto his collar.

"Can you name the feelings you are feeling?"

"I feel very sad, and ... helpless."

I gently blotted his face with a tissue, then placed it in his hand. "Be fully aware of all you are feeling as you are in the presence of your friend who has died. Let all your feelings rise to the surface, so that you can let them go, release them."

He cried silently but not motionless. Then he said, "He died. He died." And as John's voice quivered with these words, his cries became more expressive. He rubbed his closed eyes, and he swallowed deeply into his sighing chest as I suggested he let his feelings come to their full intensity.

"Get fully in touch with what you are feeling, now. Feel it within your entire self... now ask yourself why you feel helpless."

"I should have saved him." John replied with a the kind of voice that suggested feelings of guilt.

"Could you have saved him?" I questioned.

"No, I wasn't even there when it happened. But I didn't want him to die. He was my friend. I should have saved him."

"Remember the white light that is in, and around you John. Remember that you are connected to the universal love and truth, the protective light of life and love." His emotions were beginning to stabilize as I spoke. So I continued.

"Now I will count again, and on the third count, you will be on the outside looking on, watching yourself in the presence of the friend who has died. One - remembering to let all the feelings involved come to the surface. Two - knowing that you are completely safe, let the full impact of the experience come forward. And, three - you are on the outside now, looking on. Can you see yourself over there, feeling all those feelings about your friend?"

John sighed in relief as the feelings were now viewed from the outside, and he said releasing a deep breath, "Yes."

"Can you see both you and your friend, over there?"

"Yes."

"Tell me all that's going on. What's happening? What's John doing over there?"

"He's at the funeral home looking at his friend in a casket." John answered about himself, about a part of himself that he was watching experience a very painful event.

"And what is John feeling as he looks at his friend in the casket?"

"He feels very sad. But he's not crying. He's too angry to cry."

"He's enraged? Is that right?" I asked.
"Yes, he's furious. He's angry at himself because he shouldn't have let this happen. He feels that it's his fault."
"Why does he feel that it's his fault? What could he have done to stop it.?"
"I don't know. But he feels as though because he's his friend, he's responsible. He feels that he should have known and stopped it."
"How did John's friend die?"
"He took drugs." he answered flatly.
"Was John there when it happened?"
"No."
"What could John have done to stop it?"
"I can see from here that there is really nothing that John could have done. But he didn't see that."
John continued, "And even if he had been there when his friend took the drugs, would John have been responsible? Not really, because his friend would have done what he wanted to do, no matter what John did. If it didn't happen when John was around, then his friend would have done it sometime, somewhere. Hmm ... I guess that's actually what happened isn't it?'
I knew that he didn't expect me to answer his question, so I went on. "Would you like to help John?"
"Yes."
"Then face him, and ask him what he needs. Tell him that you are the universe, and that you can bring him anything and everything that he could ever want or need. Then ask him what he wants, or needs to feel better now."
I waited, as I could see the questioning going on within John while his facial muscles transformed from one expression to another. Then I asked, "What does he need?"
"He needs to know that it wasn't his fault. That no one blames him for his friend's death. He wants to stop blaming himself. He

68

needs to forgive himself. He wants to forgive
himself."

"Ah, yes, forgiveness. Giving forth." I
said. "Look at John closely. Do you love him?
Do you accept him?"

His voice was a little shaky, but very
sincere when he answered, "Yes."

"In forgiving him. What would you like
to give him?

John answered with a half-chuckle, and in
a kind of happy-cry tone, "Love, and acceptance."

"Then tell him that you don't blame him,
that no one blames him, and that you love and
accept him."

John's voice was dry and very serious,
when he said slowly and steadily, "John I don't
blame you. No one blames you. I love you. I
accept you." And tears of joy flowed easily.

"Is there anything you want to tell your
friend? Is there anything still left undone?"

John cried gently, as he spoke his love
and good-byes to his friend.

"Turn back to face yourself now John.
Are you facing yourself, now?" I asked.

"Yes."

"Would you like to reach out and embrace
yourself?"

"Yes." John answered earnestly.

"Then do so. Open your arms, and watch
yourself walk into them. Embrace yourself.
Tell yourself how much you love you. Forgive
yourself. Give forth to you the love, and
acceptance you deserve, just because you are.
Embrace yourself firmly, until you feel your-
selves merge together into one whole person.
Feel the integration. And notice how much more
of you is available now. Notice what qualities
that part of John is bringing back to you." I
gently led him through these instructions while
pacing myself with his energies, his process,
and allowing a fully complete expression of
each step.

John sighed a deep and cheerful sigh, then said, "I feel so much better. I know now that my friend's death has nothing to do with my self-worth. He didn't die to punish me, or because of me, in anyway." He sighed again and repeated, "I feel so much better!"

"Are you ready to face your friend once more?" I asked.

This time John answered excitedly, "Yes, I see him now. I love him; and I miss him, but I now feel peace with his leaving."

"Is there anything you might want to do in this immediate time in your life, that would help you bring this to full closure?" I questioned.

"Yes. I'm going to go see his parents. I wasn't able to face them before. But now I want to go tell them how much I cared for their son." he said confidently.

"Are you ready now to go back to your safe place?"

"Yes."

"One, two, and three; you are there, now. Has it changed in anyway?"

John spoke with a lighthearted voice now. "Yes, the colors are brighter. The clouds are fluffier. And I hear birds singing. And as I look out over the grass, it's a full meadow; and there are bright yellow wild flowers scattered around."

"Notice John, that since your safe place is you, and you are your safe place, that this demonstrates how much brighter, greater, and more aware your are of your own God given loveliness. How much more lovely you feel about yourself and your world."

John smiled broadly, and released a melodic "Hmmm."

"Let's look now at what has been going on in your current life John. Let's look at what's been going on with your relationships with your wife and daughter. Has anything changed for you there? What effect does this healing have on your relationship with them?"

"Interesting. I see it so differently now. I guess I was trying to run away from the closeness I got from them. I guess I was afraid that if I let them expect me to be their 'friend,' then I might fail them like I thought I had failed my old friend. I love them so much, that I didn't want to be responsible for them having any pain. I can see now that it isn't an appropriate position to hold. Also, I can see now that I deserve to have the closeness my wife and daughter offer me. I don't have to earn it or pay for it; I need only accept it, and love them back. Gees, I feel so WONDERFUL!" he shouted.

"That's great." I said, " Now be fully aware of all your new feelings, and the new depth of them. Feel the joy, the happiness, the peace, and the harmony." I paused, letting him fully experience all these wondrous feelings. Then I asked, "Are you ready now to come back?"

"Yes. I'm ready to go on with my life. I want to go see my wife and daughter right away."

"Then take all the time you need within the next fifteen seconds to feel rested, refreshed, and alive. Ask your conscious mind to reprogram; to make all your new awareness, your new cleansed self immediately available. Ask your conscious mind to reprogram; to allow you to have immediate access to your new awareness of your greatness, your brightness, and your personal and powerful light of love and life. Then come back to me in this room, fully alert within the time allowed."

I sat silently, watching John stretch, and move; getting reacquainted with his physical self in the chair he occupied; and then open his eyes and adjust to the environment the room we shared created for us.

John's first words when he was fully awake were, "Wow! That's amazing. Do you know

how powerful you are? Can you make it rain
too?!"

I chuckled softly, knowing that he had
done the work himself; and that I had only
acted as a guide as he played out his own
healing. But, I enjoyed answering his question
with a resounding "Yes, and so can you."

. . .

Going back to the root of a problem, and loving and accepting oneself through it, has expansive results. Beneath all discomfort seems to be a need for greater self-esteem, self-love, and self-acceptance.

Using the approach that our emotional problems lie within, enables us to reclaim our personal power, relieve guilt, and gain a sense of self-control which is actually the only real control that is available. Within our universe, we each have free will, and every action has a reaction within our life essence. Hence, by empowering our self-control, with LOVE, there are no limits to our health, happiness, and prosperity.

. . .

FACING AND FORGIVING

I finally found the courage to "face" the judgement I was still harboring against my mother. Mothers are human, and mine is no different. My childhood was as dysfunctional as any can be so I've had a great deal of cleaning out to do regarding suppressed emotions. The outdated emotions I was harboring toward my mother included anger, grief, resentment, and fear. We had been able to come to a reasonably functional relationship as long as I could choose to be around her when I was able to remain detached enough to interact on a more surface level. I cared about her, but I kept a wall between us that had a direct affect on the quality of our sharing.

I felt compelled to finally deal with "my" issues toward my mother. First I expressed the anger ... not in her presence of course. I found myself doing this best when I would be driving, especially during long distance drives. I would talk out loud as if to her, but into the vacant car. I'd say, "I don't need you mom!" "I'll take care of myself!" "I'll be my own mother!" Then the tears would flow. I moved in and out of the anger and depression stages repeatedly, and I was tiring of it. In my weariness I prayed for the Almighty Creator to help me let go and accept the past so that I could move on without letting it interfere with my life and happiness. Tough, so tough it is for me to let go. This is so true for so many, I find. We identify with the roles we have adopted from relationships with our parents. We identify so closely that it makes it difficult for us to release old patterns because we do not know who we will be without those familiar habits. Well, I'm certainly no exception. I was hanging on for dear life to MY IDEAS of who my mother is and how I had a right to behave in a particular way toward her.

Part of the attitude I had acquired toward Mom was due to remarks I had listened to, that I repeatedly heard from relatives who professed to be God-fearing people. When I was young I swore to myself that I would not grow up to be like the adults I saw as being critical, judging and unforgiving. So I **talked** forgiveness -A LOT! But I didn't really know how to do it. I had not seen it done. I had no model, no example to follow. Even though I swore not to grow up judging, and critical and unforgiving, that's just what I had done! I had ideas of what I wanted my mother to be like, or at least what I thought any good mother should be like. From that premise I evaluated and judged my mother against this fairy tale type of mother image I had set in my mind. You would think when my daughter went through a stage of judging me in the same fashion, it would have "clicked" for me to notice how I was treating my own mother. But no, I was still too dense. Yes, "dense" in the sense that my walls were so thick that the insights couldn't penetrate through to my heart.

There is a dear sweet and tender man named Jerry who has taught me more about loving. He touches me with such warmth and respect that there is nothing I can do outside of melting. He strokes my face like it's the silky fur of a newborn kitten. His words are few, and yet he says so much! I talk and talk, rambling on and on, taking up so much time and making so much noise trying to share the tenderness that I must first uncover. Yet this sweet, gentle man speaks with depth, breadth, and volume with a simple touch. What a gift! What a blessing he is!

I died and felt the full impact of love and acceptance throughout my whole being. Now when an occasion occurs, like when Jerry **touches** my face with such genuine tenderness, it touches my innermost true self. When this happens it reminds me that it doesn't take courage, but **FAITH** to move through old fears. Old fears that are no longer useful or appropriate in the life of happiness I am now in the process of painting for myself. Life truly can be heaven when we stop bracing ourself against its unpredictable experiences. Forgiveness and acceptance truly are the means to peace, joy, and love. Let me share how it happened with my mother.

I had just spent some time with this special man Jerry, and I was still savoring the beauty of the honest and open caring. I was in the little northern Michigan town of Gaylord, which is only 49 miles from the even smaller town of Hillman, Michigan where my mother lives. My conscience was gnawing at me since I hadn't called or written to her in quite some time - not even since I had received her birthday wishes with a note saying she hadn't heard from anyone in awhile. The guilt I was dumping upon myself had reached a level of intolerance, so I decided to give her a quick call and say hello. "Hello" was all I intended to offer along with my excuses for not having been in touch sooner. After doing several unnecessary little household chores to procrastinate, a little voice in me said, "CALL NOW!" I went to the phone and dialed.

"Hello Mom." I said.

"Mary ... Oh Mary ... I'm so glad you

called!" I heard her say with such emotion that I couldn't completely maintain my old habit of detaching.

"Hi Mom, I'm sorry I haven't called sooner but I've been very busy working. As a matter of fact I'm working down state for a couple of weeks. I just happened to come up to Gaylord to visit a friend, so I thought I would call you for a minute." I was rambling on and on with my apology and my position of only being able to talk for a minute. I was trying to keep control of the situation so that I could stay removed from feeling any emotions with my own mother.

When I finished with my matter-of-fact statement, she excitedly said, "You're only 40 miles away, please come over!"

Again I heard a tenderness and emotion I couldn't remember hearing from her quite the same before. I suppose it was my way of listening that had changed, rather than her way of talking. But even noticing this tenderness in her voice, I still found I had some resistance left, so I said, "I really need to use some self-discipline and do some writing today. Besides it's snowing and the roads probably aren't too good."

Mom persisted in an almost pleading voice now, "Do you have to do your work there? Couldn't you do it here? Please come over, there's a little snow, but the roads won't be bad. Please come over."

My walls started tumbling down. I really didn't want to hold them up any longer. Her sincere request was just what I needed to hear to find enough sense of safety to move through all the old baggage. "Ok." I said. "We can have lunch." I was accepting her invitation, but that stubborn part of me still tried to keep it as if it were a casual friend I was meeting for lunch as I was passing through the area. Boy oh boy, can I be stubborn! I had vowed as a young child that once I became an adult I would be in charge, and no one would ever get the best of me again. That was such a SELF-destructive position. It had been undermining my ability to have close relationships all my life. I am so thankful for dying to remember, and so thankful for the Almighty Creator giving me experiences like Jerry's touch to open me up again.

I got into the car and started the trip on a snowy northern Michigan road. Although I was driving a treacherous wintry, winding, slippery road through huge snow flakes that reduced visibility, my thoughts were moving along a much more wonderful path. I first started thinking that this is my opportunity to forgive my mother. I'll go to her, I thought, and tell her that I forgive her for all her mistakes, and redeem her from the guilt of causing me so many pains. Then as I listened to my arrogant thoughts, I knew that it was me that needed forgiving. It was me who was in error. It was me who was judging, and criticizing. I was the one who was not accepting as the Almighty Creator accepted me and all my flaws in the black and brilliantly lit space. I was the one who needed to forgive, and be forgiven. Tears washed the mascara from my lashes, and my eyes were red as I stopped at the village florist on my way to my Mom's apartment. I wanted to give Mom a peace offering - something that represented my new way of relating to her - my acceptance of her, and my desire to be a daughter to her again, while letting her be a mother to me. I took the flower arrangement to her with a card on which I had written, "Thank you for giving birth to my life. I love you. Mary." As I carried it into her home and handed it to her, I felt like a little girl taking wild flowers to her sweet mother. These were feelings I had been denying myself for so many years, and now I was FINALLY ready to let them be a part of my life again. Such a miracle I was feeling.

When I walked in and saw in Mom's face that she knew this was an important moment, it made things a little easier for me. She opened her arms to me and I moved into her embrace and sobbed on her shoulder. When I was once again composed enough to speak, I told her I had to tell her quick while I had the courage. "I thought I needed to forgive you Mom for all your mistakes in mothering me. But now I realize that I hope you can forgive me for judging you. I have been so resentful and angry. I'm so sorry."

Her words were so comforting. At first I thought she was about to say that I didn't need to be forgiven and that it was no big deal. But I think she could see that I truly needed her forgiveness, and she gave it. I felt cleansed, lightened, and so fatigued as I listened to her tell me how much she loves me. We told each other that we wanted to be mother and daughter. Mom suggested that we let go of the past and begin with this very moment in love. It was so beautiful! These words cannot capture the rapture of the loving we finally exchanged. I had been a 44 year old brat, trying to make my mother act the way I wanted her to act. No longer. I now held her in my embrace and stroked her face and hair with a touch of tenderness I hadn't known before. In accepting my mother's humanness I feel that I have accepted my own womanly humanness.

Actually, on the outside of this life's illusion where I was with the Almighty Creator, forgiveness isn't even necessary because judgement doesn't exist in the Black and Brilliant God/Love space. Acceptance is infinite, and is not a part of time. Time, like all other things in this reality, is a component of the collective thinking of boundaries and separation that are a part of the laws of this reality. Since we agree to live within the laws of this reality in order to be gifted with its characteristics, then forgiveness is an essential part of living in happiness here.

Remembering and acting on the faith that will enable you to free yourself from your own self-imposed prison of fear is a miracle. Even if the external objects or people don't respond with the love and openness that my mother did, it is you the forgiver, who is receiving the cleansing by the offering of the forgiveness. So, even without a response at all, one can release the binds that hold us to an untruth of non-acceptance. I forgive me, and I feel heavenly for it.

I pray that in sharing this experience on these pages, it will act as a touch of tenderness on your face, and on your heart, to let go - let go and LOVE.

CONTROL

Control!
Control?
Positive or negative?
Con the Trol?
Trol the Con?
Trying to control others or external forces,
  is an effort to Con the Trol.
Controlling ourselves is Trolling the Con.
When we feel out of control
      there is pain and panic.
When we feel in control,
      we feel worthwhile and successful.
When we feel controlled,
      we feel manipulated and angry,
           even weak.
When we feel controlling,
      we feel powerful and dominating;
      we feel others are weaker than us.
The only good control is awareness.
Awareness which leads to choices,
      with integrity.
Choices - not control - brings **HAPPINESS**!

BRUCE

It was a warm September day when Bruce came to my office and completed my intake form by answering the following question: What is the reason you have sought assistance from Dr. McMurray? (What are your goals?) His answer was simply: Clear up my confusion and mixed up thoughts. Bruce was separated from his wife of eleven years, and even though it had been his choice to initiate the separation, he was distraught, tense, and confused. Here was a man who had been working hard for many years to earn a career as a doctor, and he was now enjoying a thriving practice in chiropractic medicine. For years he had felt "below" his wife (who held an important and highly paid job), while she helped him obtain necessary degrees and establish his growing practice. He had a wife, a very satisfying career, and two wonderful children who are very important to him. It would seem that he would have the world by the tail, but instead he was sitting in my office telling me that his world was upside down, and very unhappy. He spent years longing, and doing without, as he struggled to achieve success according to his own criteria. This feeling of longing, and struggling to obtain what always seemed to be "elusive" dreams was a pattern that had been set long before he even met his wife, had his children, or started his climb to a satisfying career. When he had "arrived," so to speak, he sat back and saw all that he had. That's when the deep

confusion set in. Instead of relaxing and enjoying the rewards of his efforts, he became
aware of a dissatisfaction in his most personal
relationship (with his wife). He became critical of her, and even called her controlling.
He decided that he wanted to be less dependent
upon her, and more in control of his own life.
So he began doing things he had long wanted to
do but hadn't done, because of his previous
fear of upsetting and loosing his wife. After
inviting her to join him, and hearing her re-
fusal, he started going out, listening to
music, talking to others, making new friend-
ships. He was looking for a deeper, more real
feeling of happiness. The "things" that were
supposed to mean happiness, didn't have the
depth he was searching for. At this crisis
point he was ready to experience the feelings
he had buried many years earlier, as a means of
surviving in a world that was frightening, and
very demanding. He had reached a point of
readiness. He was ready to truly feel love in
the depths of his being. He wanted it as much
as life itself. Hence he came to my office
looking for a means to accomplish his ultimate
goal.

Bruce and his wife had seen a counselor
together prior to Bruce coming to visit me.
In those former therapy sessions, the therapist
made an evaluation of the relationship, and
based on their childhood experiences, told the
couple that their problems were due to the fact
that Mrs. Bruce was an Adult Child of an Alco-
holic. The therapist had diagnosed Bruce's
wife as coming from a dysfunctional home and
being dysfunctional herself. However, overlooked was the fact that Bruce was a counter-
part of the current dysfunctional relationship
with his wife. By not looking at Bruce's part
in the situation he was enabled to continue to
see his world as being controlled by external
things. Bruce reacted to this by pulling
further away from his wife, because he had been

encouraged to continue blaming his wife for his problems, for his PERSONAL unhappiness. He became even more determined to make some decisions based on his own feelings rather than on the needs of others. He was unable to get in touch with his own feelings, which would be something new for him. So, he withdrew even further from responsibility. (Responsibility simply means "the ability to respond.") He had tried to find happiness by looking to a new relationship (again with the attitude that happiness could be provided from an external source). As a result, he felt disoriented and confused. His confusion and fear grew greater and greater. The first therapist's external approach to problem solving, along with Bruce's own attempts at finding happiness from outside, accentuated his already low self-esteem. It suggested that the power over his life was outside of him, so his panic grew. In his own words he felt, "out of control."

When Bruce shared his story with me I told him that it was possible for him to feel happiness because happiness came from within. I suggested that it was possible to become happy, and peaceful by directing ones attentions on oneself, regardless of what others around chose to do. We discussed various methods of therapy. When I described my favorite method of using deep relaxation to go directly to the source, the root, of the discomfort he quickly agreed to it feeling confident that it would expedite his healing, his growth.

In deep relaxation and guided imagery Bruce and I took his inner child (embraced by safety) back to the root of some perceived traumas from his younger years. It was a beautiful process (much like John's) in which we repeatedly took Bruce to situations he could heal with love. Over and over we had him step outside of experiences and love himself through it. We were able to create an opportunity for

85

Bruce to see his history with a more mature, universal love perspective which released great fear from his belief system.

Bruce was not able to turn his marriage into what he longed for and it has since dissolved However, he has drawn out from within himself the natural ability to create his own happiness. In the marriage, there were TWO free-wills at work, and Bruce only had control of his own. He is now in charge of his own. He is at peace with himself, while peacefully raising his two sons as a single parent. His chiropractic practice is flourishing and secure. He is now aware of his personal power which is a direct descendent of the Almighty Creative Power. In his life Bruce still encounters challenges. But now he handles them with self-esteem, and serenity since he is honest with himself, and true to himself. Being true to himself includes remembering from whence he comes. This creates a life in which the original love source has a direct affect on his choices and results. Peace is a more frequent friend for Bruce today.

. . .

I can sincerely identify with Bruce. There have been times in my life when deeply buried, OLD mis-perceived fears, have caused me to act in many backward ways. Arrogance is a cloak I have tried on, along with the garb of denial, control, anger, and depression. I spent some years believing that there were things beyond my control that I needed to MAKE different by MY OWN efforts. I am so thankful that now I am learning to more frequently and consistently have the faith to remember that "all there is, is love, love is all there is." When I remember this, I not only receive and experience love for myself, but I freely, and very joyfully offer and share love fully. When I am in tune with my true reality (The Love of the Almighty Creator) life is awesomely and breathtakingly WONDERFUL. I see the word "wonderful" as meaning "Full of Wonder."

Can you imagine how Full of Wonder, and full of LOVE, the world would be if everyone could allow the love to shine through more often? I pray for each and every one of us to relax, let go, and let the truth be KNOWN.

LOOK INWARD ANGEL

All you need
        is in your soul,
Where Love, God, resides.
Depend on you,
        the best friend
You will ever have.
Listen
        to your heart,
Your feelings.
Seek Quiet.
Seek Peace.
Seek Aloneness.
Accept you, wonderful you.
Meditate.
Accept the messages
        from within.
God talks through your soul.
Your soul talks through your
        feelings, your mind, your body.,
Listen ...
For profound, yet simple
        answers.
Look inward, Angel.

"Raggs' Riches"

I wanted to do an article on clowns. So I asked various clowns from the Shrine Clown Unit for interviews. As I did, I kept hearing them say "If you really want to get to the heart of clowning, talk to Dave Florida a.k.a. "Raggs".

One clown named Packy says, "Raggs makes it happen." Another, Chuckles, says, "Dave Florida (Raggs) is like a big brother to me. He is strong, yet he's not afraid to shed real tears, and feel openly. I have a lot of respect for that man."

These were pretty wonderful things to say about someone, so I decided not to linger, and go to the big guy. I called Raggs and told him about the article I wanted to write about clowning. I said I wanted to expose the "people behind the paint," and find out what kind of people become clowns. I also wanted to know why they clowned, and what everyone gets out of it, including the clowns themselves.

When I told Dave that I had been repeatedly told that he was the epitome of a clown from the inside out, he expressed embarrassment, a hint of shyness. At the same time I heard in his voice a "Thank you" for noticing the efforts, infinite as they are, that he contributes to the beauty and love that clowning expresses.

In our initial phone conversation I heard Raggs say things like, "Charity is the giving of a little by many to help a special few with a special cause or problem no matter what race, creed, or color ... Clowning is an act of love ... Charity is all of us"; "mankind has the ability to be greedy, but we give to fill our sense of responsibility"; and "you can't run out of love." Hearing these remarkable remarks made me more and more enthusiastic about meeting this man. I was really looking forward to our upcoming interview, since he had already touched my heart.

When I arrived at the scheduled restaurant, Raggs, a big man, was casually seated in a booth wearing a soft smile on his full face. No introductions were necessary, although I reached out my hand and received a strong yet gentle shake. The conversation poured out easily and instantly, like the nourishment of the lunch we were sharing. I asked about clowns, and clowning, but the words and "worlds" shared reached far beyond the few questions I had come prepared to ask. Raggs had a few of his own questions for me. For example he asked if significant others in my life had a hard time confining me, and when I answered affirmatively, he asked "So the twinkle in your eyes is your own, isn't it?"

I knew immediately that Raggs was not only a big man, but a sensitive and alert man as well.

We talked about the Sneaker Fund, a project for which Dave is the Ambassador. The donations made to this fund are for buying footwear for children in the International Shrine Clowns Burns Institutes. Raggs not only manages this project, but he motivates, promotes, coordinates, and gives of himself and his own funds to help it continually reach beyond past successes.

I asked Raggs about his own personal motivation for giving so much of himself and he told me a story from his past. "When I was 13," he said, "my father died, and I was told that boys don't cry. But I said, 'bullshit' and I cried. I decided that something good would come from my father's death. So I have spent the rest of my life working to live up to the saint-like person my father was often described as."

We talked about crying, and how it was a natural human experience and Dave says that "crying is a cleansing part of you that has to be expressed or it comes out in a form of physical damage." We discussed how in our world people often hide their real intimate loving self behind the many roles society asks them to play and Raggs' remark on this was, "People often clown to allow their real personality to come out, the part of them that is god-like."

Noticing a spiritual trend to our conversation I shared with Raggs the death experience I had in an automobile accident in February of 1988. He immediately shared with me that he'd experienced the same "heaven, or non/all space" I talked of, and he'd experienced it not once, but twice.

Raggs told me, "When I was a small child I had a dream that I fell off the earth and into forever. At the point where it all stopped (the earth) it was all just plain good and nothing else to it. There's no words to describe it." I identified with what Raggs was saying and added, with Raggs' agreement, that this space/place had no lines of definition or boundariers, but all was infinitely united in love.

He then went on to tell me, "Then another time I was laying still on a dock in the summertime watching the clouds in the sky, and I realized that I felt not bad, not good, not angry, not happy, not anything, but I just WAS. I felt serene and totally and completely just here, and I really KNEW IT. I just was and shall EVER BE. And that was a time for being a perfect "non," an eclipse. Perfect feelings of infinity, peacefully." We went on to talk about how if we could all remember - all the time - that in every moment we are this infinite oneness then as Raggs says, "we would be at peace and know."

"We get caught up in our physical existence." Raggs says. But this led him into an appreciation of the human (physical experience) because he asked me, "At what age did you discover that it really was exciting to experience this communicating with other human beings?" As I was forming my answer he went on to say, "To exchange words, ideas, and thoughts and not be afraid. To say to you that it's alright for you to express yourself whether you're right or wrong. I so often stress in meeting after meeting to my brothers, the other clowns, that it's ok to say what you think, and it's more important than whether you're right or wrong, or I'm right or wrong. What's important is that we attempt to share." Raggs also says that this communication is part of a need to belong, to be accepted. With this remark I admitted that I'm still working on letting go of what I see as a need to defend my position. Raggs' answer to this was "I think you'll always be doing it because you're tied to confinements, rules, regulations, morals, anything and everything that's part of this world. That's where the word responsibility comes in, you're tied to it whether you want to be or not."

At this point I couldn't help saying, "No wonder Chuckles looks up to you as his big brother." I found myself opening up to Raggs and telling him about a recent regrettable experience in which I was still trying to exercise my personal control beyond myself and onto a friend. I told Raggs that I was still learning to remember more consistently that I could relax and let go; let go and trust the truth of the universe - that truth being that the Almighty Creator/Love will be there fully and completely constantly and consistently as

92

long as we get our personal ego ideas out of the way. Raggs' comforting words were "You were in a state of transition, and growth, and your enthusiasm flowed. It's ok." he said. Raggs' loving responses were consistent, and steady because he said in many ways: "It's OK, just be." In agreement I said, "Yes I was overly enthusiastic, but with hindsight being what it is, I also love my friend right where my friend is in his own soul/psyche development. Again Raggs' simple answer seemed profound, "That's because you SEE him."

Well, I have the distinct feeling that Raggs SEES more than most, because he pauses to look, and look with his heart. He says, "Life is really quite simple if you look at everything as black and white, but if you start to look INTO it then you find things out." So I added, "So black and white is sort of like, 'ignorance is bliss.'"

Raggs looks and sees not only with his eyes but with far more. He not only notices, but he acts with love on what he sees.

Those acts of love take the form of circus performances, parades, festivals, mini clinics for hurt and crippled children, clinics that lead to major programs in which the clown unit adopts said children and cares for them financially and otherwise, and it even takes the form of coloring books.

Clowns ... each of them are as different and unique as each individual is different. It doesn't matter whether they are a white-face clown like Ronald McDonald, an Auguse clown with a combination of three or four colors added to a white face, a character clown taking from the theme of a famous clown like Emmet Kelly, or a Bum Clown in rags, clowns are adults who dress up in crazy clothes, bright colors, big noses, weird wigs, two-foot long shoes, have pockets full of balloons, and have funny faces; and they speak from big hearts.

Dave says that when he teaches someone to

93

be a clown he tells them to, "Let yourself go. Let yourself be free to be the person you perceive yourself to be. I ask them what do you want to be? What is in your mind? What character are you? What colors are you? What do you look like?" These sound to me like excellent questions for anyone to ask himself/herself, especially if one wants to be the most he/she is capable of being at any given moment.

Clowns go out "giving a little by many to help a special few with a special cause." For this I'd like to shout a resounding "THANKS!" to all the clowns of Dave Florida's (Raggs') clown unit, and all the clowns around the world. I would especially like to offer a heartfelt "Thank you!" to Mr. Dave Florida, a.k.a. Raggs, for being who he really is: a christ-like, loving creature, and for sharing who he is with myself among the many.

Raggs is a very rich man - rich in love. And he is the epitome of clowning. He is a big man, who as a bum clown, lets a huge heart shine from beneath the rags he wears while he speaks of an issue very dear to my heart: We are all of the one LIGHT -Love. I don't believe he was just "clowning around" when he said, "Mankind invented time. Before that there was just Eternity."

INSIGHT

Insight
     is awareness
         of your
             internal vision.

Look inside
     where your angel lives.

See Truth.

See Love.

See Eternally.

Natural

Since death, and rebirth, I have felt more aligned with the Almighty Creator/Love's non-judgmental and all accepting truth. Being even more open-minded than ever, I found that opportunities and experiences to realize this became more available to me. These types of experiences are reminders to Live and Let Live. The following story is true, and it is one I was hesitant to include here. But, it is honest; and I feel it has value in bringing comfort to millions who share the perspective I found in the following experience.

. . .

I drove down the highway pressing beyond the speed limit because I had left late for a very important date. I was certain I knew the way. So certain that I overlooked the sign for my exit. My certainty was certainly in error.

I had left home heading for the Whispering Oaks nudists resort. I was to be a guest of a friend ... a new experience for me.

It was easy to convince myself that missing the exit was fate telling me that nudism wasn't meant for me today. So I went home, sat down with a book and told myself that If I had gone I would have been running away from myself because it was really meant for me to have a day of solitude - BUNK!

Besides July 8, and 9 was National Nudism

97

Weekend, so I wanted to see for myself what it's all about. Two hours later I started out again, this time arriving at the gate of the resort alone - since it was too late to connect with my friend Dan. By now I was so determined to go through with it that I persevered in pressing the gate intercom button at least eight times before I heard a relaxed male voice say, "Hello there," through the small metal speaker.

I confidently said, "I'm a visitor, a friend of Dan's. May I come in?"

"Sure," said the anonymous male voice. "Come on in. Stop at the office and I'll show you around."

I drove through the gate as if I was driving into any park, not really thinking about what I was about to see and experience. It all felt very NATURAL now that I had spent my anxiety in two hours of procrastination. I parked next to a couple of golf carts and got out of my car. I was greeted by a man wearing only a shirt. "Hi, I'm Gary, maybe I can find Dan for you." Gary turned toward the lawn where numerous people were sunbathing. Just then Dan started walking toward us. "Does Dan wear a white hat?" Gary asked with a little lighthearted lilt in his voice. "I guess he does," I said, since that was all he was wearing. I was feeling at least a smidgen of uneasiness at this point, but my discomfort was dissolving as quickly as it came because the atmosphere was definitely easy, NATURAL, light, comfortable and confident.

While Dan showed me where to leave my car for the afternoon he told me that as I came through the security gates at Whispering Oaks I had left the "textile world," as nudists would say. But he also reassured me that although practicing nudists enjoy being as natural as a newborn, they are also practical. "For example," Dan said, "we wear clothes when frying bacon."

As I walked from my car to begin my tour,
I immediately felt out of place in my shorts
and t-shirt. Dan must have read my mind because he said, "When you're ready, you'll
probably be more comfortable if you take your
clothes off."

"I need a little time, okay." I returned
with a slightly nervous giggle.

As we walked in the sunshine and cool
breezes I saw green trees, a small pond,
breasts bouncing on the volleyball court,
sunburned derrieres, a blue water pool, and
bare-skinned babes playing ball.

By the time we reached the club house, I
was feeling more and more like I was wearing an
eskimo parka on Waikiki beach. My simple,
light cotton shorts and top had begun to feel
weighty.   In the club house was a large hot
tub. "Now here's something I'm more comfortable with." I thought to myself. Since I had
had a couple of occasions to skinny-dip in a
private hot tub in my past, I decided that this
would be the most comfortable place to take the
plunge into nudism. I pretended that I was in
the home of a friend, undressed, laid my "textiles" on a chair, and haughtily stepped down
into the hot steamy water. The haughtiness was
an act, but it got me through the gateway into
my first adventure with nudism.   At first I
imagined that the water veiled my NATURAL way,
but my fears quickly melted with the warmth of
the water, the people, the place, and the
general atmosphere.

We continued my tour, and I was pleased
to find canoeing, swimming, fishing, nature
trails, tennis, volleyball, and a softball
field. I also saw, just as naturally, tennis
shoes and tatoos, sunglasses and bare ..., gold
chains and flip-flop shower shoes, softballs -
volleyballs - tennis balls - and others, bath-
ing bodies in the open air, a man and woman
showering on the porch - sudsing and rinsing
the residue of the day as naturally as the rain

washes the dust from the flower and quenches its thirst.

I saw a striped sunburn running vertically from head to toe from not turning over, an appendectomy scar, the tender flesh of a sweet innocent little girl climbing the stairs of a slide on the playground, and yellow and red life jackets above oars resting on bare cool thighs in the summer sun.

I saw Lincoln Continentals, golf carts, Ford pick-ups, a fish-stocked pond, a wooden bridge, mosquitos biting where you can't itch, baseball caps and nude naps on the green grass with a bonnie lass, fishing poles in the watering holes held by little boys feeling the freedom of the NATURAL spirit, and a sign that read "SPEED LIMIT 5."

I saw tents, umbrellas, trailers (permanent and transient), family picnics, and the American Flag waved strongly on the hill above it all.

I met Lloyd, an 80 year old man who has been enjoying the freedom of nudism at this particular park since 1971. Lloyd says, "It's all quite proper, you know."

I met Sandy and Dave who say they took to nudism NATURALLY. It's first names only here, a natural respect for privacy.

I shared the hot tub with 7 or 8 young people ages 9 to 14 who bared it all, from the chatter of sports to their own natural selves as comfortably as a bee nourishes itself with the nectar of a wild Iris.

I heard someone ask, "Have you seen Sharon?" and the response was "I'm not sure, what color is her towel?"

Best of all I hugged a tree and embraced the bark of a 60 foot oak. A tree, one of God's "natural" creations. A tree grows from the inside out while it's firmly rooted and reaching into the heavens at the same time. A tree ... a tree is as natural as me.

As I stood in the parking lot and dressed

100

by my car I realized the relaxed freedom I'd felt for the past several hours, and "textiles" now seemed more functional than social to me.

After moving through my fears, I found the courage to experience a natural happening. These were families who were raising their children to accept their bodies as beautiful, and natural creations of the Almighty Creative Love. They had avoided programming their children with negative and fearful thoughts and inhibitions about the totally natural vehicle the Almighty Creator has given them to embellish life with - their bodies.

When I drove out the gate I was thankful that I had moved beyond my world of rigidity and resistance and into a world of nature and nudism.

"... and the American Flag waved strongly on the hill above it all."

LETTING GO

I just sat down to dinner when the phone rang. I got up, went to the kitchen counter, picked up the phone, and brought it back to the table.

"Hello." I said.

"Hello Mary, this is Helen."

"Oh, hello Helen, I almost called you a couple of days ago. I was wondering what's happening with the sale of the lot."

"Well, that's what I'm calling about." Helen, my real estate agent, answered. "We'll have the closing in about two weeks."

We went on to talk about the particulars regarding the selling of the last asset that was jointly owned by myself and my ex-husband. It was a small parcel of land, with only a small monetary value, but the significance of disolving the "final" link between me and a major chapter of my life shook me up.

My thoughts went back in time and I remembered ...

...

I felt the car dip slightly as it rolled over a patch of gravel and earth before leveling off and rolling onto the concrete driveway. I pushed the romote control button for the garage door opener and waited for the large wooden double door to open. I could hear the hum of the motor as the door lifted. I moved slowly into the garage I had driven into hundreds of times over the past 18 years. As I opened the car door it seemed heavier than it ever had before. I got out of the car and stood on the painted concrete floor and looked around. There were still a few thumb tacks in the walls from where we had hung pictures of each of our daughters when we had held their open-house parties for high-school graduation in this garage. My "baby" (the youngest of my two daughters) had just graduated three months earlier, and I could remember the event as if it were today. Not only had my baby, Tina, graduated from high school, but I had this very moment arrived home after driving her to Michigan State University where she was beginning her freshmen year in college. Her older sister, Lisa had moved away from home almost two years earlier, and their father had left just prior to Lisa, and shortly after the automobile accident in which I experienced death. Within two years the house had emptied. Here I was, beyond the divorce of a twenty-two year marriage, and standing in the garage of the empty house where I had spent the last 18 years raising a family. I went to the door that would open up to the family room. I stood on a small concrete step with my hand on the textured metal door knob, and froze. I felt numb. When I finally went in, I walked through the rooms of the now vacant, hollow house, and sobbed out loud, "Hello, nobody!" Tears ran down my already puffy cheeks. I had cried during most of the one hour drive from MSU to "home" after leaving Tina at college.

My heart swelled as I wandered through the empty house. It really was just a house now. The family that had made it "home" had dispersed. I stood in the kitchen where I had wiped noses, permed Lisa's hair, canned hundreds of quarts of vegetables and fruits, watched Tina tap dance, and prepared nearly 20,000 meals. I stood at the sink and looked out the window at the spacious backyard. The backyard - in 18 years I'd seen the girls swing from their knees on the side of the swing-set; a bouncy handful of black labrador puppy grow to the old age of 17 with gray whiskers and wobbly legs; and a dozen or more spruce trees grow from 18 inches to over 20 feet high. We had had cookouts, graduation parties, firework watches, croquet games, sunbathing, splashes in tiny swimming pools, magnolia blossoms, irises, roses, snowmen, and snowball fights in this backyard.

I turned from the kitchen window and looked into the small attached dining room. I could see birthday cakes on the table and realized that between the four of us we had celebrated approximately 72 birthdays here. That's a lot of cake and ice cream! We had eaten goulash, B.L.T.'s, steak, stew, turkey, tuna, and chinese on the round table centered in the tiny room allowing just enough space for the chairs to surround it. We had also done schoolwork, paintings, and sewing patterns on this table. Major decisions, and stand-offs occurred between the walls of this dining room.

As I walked out of the dining room I moved into the hall where the laundry facilities were. "Oh my God!" I thought. "How much has passed through these machines!" Diapers, costumes, blue-jeans, and frilly dresses were but a few of the thousands of garments that were renewed here.

On down the hall were the bedrooms. I peeked into each of the girl's rooms and almost melted with the memories. I remembered the many colors that had decorated each of their rooms. The girl's bathroom was packed full of the past. We had treated chicken pox there, and primped for the prom years later.

Then there was the master bedroom. The

master bedroom had seen passion, cold wars, and everything in between. The window gave view to the backyard shaded by a large oak tree. Under that oak tree was where I had gone on hot summer days for solitude, rest and studying. Under the oak tree was my place to get rooted, centered, and refreshed - except in January or February when the snow might be more than a foot deep. Then the spacious living room in the front of the house was my retreat. It was decorated with soft blues and whites, and it had a large fireplace that didn't hold nearly enough fires to suit me. I had just begun to build fires rather regularly in the last few years, especially since the family was falling apart. The fire seemed to warm me from the inside out as I would often stare into the flames peacefully. The living room had mostly been "my" room because the rest of the family spent most of their time in the "family-room" where the television was.

"Oh yes, the television." They would turn the T.V. on as they walked past it coming in the door - even if they kept on going and didn't even sit down to watch it. I can't count how many times I turned it off behind them before they could get caught up in it. The television sat in the built-in bookcases and cabinets that covered the end wall of the family-room. Ah, yes, the cabinets. They were filled with photos that represented multitudes of magnificent memories. Magnificent? Yes, mostly - for many years. But not the recent ones.

A beautiful romance had gone sour. It had turned from being loving, accepting and supporting to judging, criticizing, and projecting unrealistic expectations onto one another.

I sat down in the easy chair in the family-room, feeling extremely exhausted. The pain in my heart was excruciating. I felt like my chest would split open and spill out all over the room. The family I had dreamed of and worked so hard to create, was gone. I was alone in the room; in the house and it felt like I was totally alone in the world. My instincts told me to reach out; to ask for help and support. I was a total mess!

Through tears, I struggled to find phone numbers for friends in directories, on slips of paper and on business cards. After several sobbing calls I found someone to come and stay with me for the night. I felt I couldn't bear to be alone and after conversation with friends in the psychological field, I decided I needed some concentrated help to get me on my feet again.

I had seen enough dysfunction in my past marriage to know I still had work to do in the area of "codependency."

An explanation may be necessary here, for readers who are not familiar with the term codependent.

When Melody Beattie answered the question, "What is codependency?" in her book, CODEPENDENT NO MORE, she used the following quotes from Robert Subby's book, CODEPENDENCY - AN EMERGING ISSUE, where he stated that "codependency is: An emotional, psychological, and behavioral condition that develops as a result of an individual's prolonged exposure to, and practice of, a set of oppressive rules — rules which prevent the open expression of feelings as well as the direct discussion of personal and interpersonal problems."

Ernie Larsen, another codependency expert, defines codependency as:

Those self-defeating, learned

*behaviors or character defects that
results in a diminished capacity to
initiate or to participate in loving relationships.*

I like these definitions since they are
not limited to describing only the results from
chemically dependent relationships. I like the
broad definitions which allow for the inclusion
of many learning environments that can result
in the same or similar results as described.
I use the word "co-dependency" cautious-
ly. I'm not really thrilled with the term
since it can be confusing, and it has many
negative connotations attached to it. I
actually feel that to co-depend can be healthy
if it's in BALANCE. We co-create and we co-
depend in order to co-create collective experiences, but the jargon of the day is to say that
interdependency is the better choice over co-
dependency. The term interdependency is used
in other literature with much the same meaning
I am suggesting the BALANCING co-dependency
would mean. To be interdependent means to
recognize the inclusive necessity to cooperate
with all other factors (peo-ple, places, and
things) to create or cohabitate collective
environments and experiences.

GEORGIA ON MY MIND

The process of letting go described in the last chapter was a catalyst for moving into deeper healing experiences. After doing an honest inventory of my personal condition, I began researching facilities around the country that offered intensive in-house treatment for co-dependency. I chose a wonderful place in Georgia. As I was preparing for the trip, I realized that although I was frightened, I was looking forward to sharing a week with a specific consistent small group of people day and night. I heard myself thinking that I wouldn't be "alone." I would have "family." You see, I had placed so much importance on the family system, that I felt unsure about functioning without one. I was feeling that I'd rather have the past family back even if it was predictably unhealthy.

I packed comfy clothes and a stuffed animal as directed by the facility, and nervously flew off to Georgia. When Dr. Mendini interviewed me during my intake into the facility, I told him how insecure and inadequate I was feeling; and how I felt uncertain about my own career as a psychologist. I said that I needed to take care of myself first, and put taking care of others on a back burner. I felt scattered and uneasy about making decisions regarding my future. I had a blank canvas in front of me, and I was having trouble picking up a brush and applying the first strokes of color and form to my new life. All I knew was that I didn't want to be "alone."

Although my near-death-experience had been a reminder that I was never alone, there was old programming in my systems (memory in my cells) that still needed to be retaught. The empty house triggered reactions in me that were illustrative of the systems from my accumulated **experiences**. Experiences like those described in the August 1949 chapter were part of the programming that was in mind, and made up the accumulated belief system I currently had to operate from. I knew in my head and my heart that the experience did not define "who" I was, but old tapes were causing me to act out old habits. I went to Georgia to change the tapes and to rewrite my interpretations of the past experiences. I needed to have an opportunity to express pent up emotions that, as a child, I was unable to understand, or express fully.

During the week-long treatment, extensive progress was made. I had an opportunity to release **LOTS** of buried emotion. I especially benefited from releasing the anger I had previously not been able to give myself permission to release. This was extremely helpful. We were set up as a family, and told that the six of us in our group were our "family of choice," rather than our "family of origin." The role modeling, and family sculpturing was a profound experience. In the family sculpturing each of us took turns having our group members stand in for significant players in our pasts experiences. We were then able to finally act out the reactions that we had previously buried. It was an excellent catalyst for tapping into emotions that had been locked away for a long, long time. In some cases we purged anger, fear, and grief that was thirty or forty years old.

The week's experiences helped me to "remember" exactly what I needed in order to move ahead with my life confidently, and successfully. I learned that as I was living with people whom I did not choose, it suggested a similar family situation as in my youth. I was mandated to rely solely upon the members of my group as my "family" even though they weren't necessarily in synchronization with me - my perspectives, interests, desires, needs, or style. It became completely clear to me that the picture I currently wanted to paint of my life was different from what externally designated "authorities" thought was in my best interest. It was also clear to me that along with claiming my freedom to choose what "I" wanted for "me," I was also maturing emotionally. This new maturation enabled me to feel confident about making decisions and commitments which "I" decided were in my best interest. The members of my group, my "family of choice" for the week in Georgia, are beautiful people. Each and everyone of them are beautiful in their own right - just as beautiful as myself and everyone else equally. But the specifics of the individual characteristics did not fit into the new picture I was selecting to paint on my new canvas of life. I left a great deal of old baggage behind when I left Georgia, and yet there's still more for me to sort through. I continue to work on issues as they are unlocked or rise to the surface.

However, as the week progressed in Georgia, so did my independence and confidence. The more independence and specific individualization I felt and displayed, the more I was being ostracized by the group. I was setting my own personal boundaries. I was defining my personal world and, how I wanted to experience it. I was no longer feeling that I wanted, or needed to feel dependent on the opinions of others in order to define/create an "acceptable" life. In the beginning of the week I was looking at everyone, and their behaviors, for clues as to how to act in order to be an accepted member of the group. By the end of the week, I was defining very clearly who I was, and what I wanted my life to look like and feel like. I was setting healthy boundaries. They were also defining their own boundaries, even if we differed in our choices. This only came after a week of each of us in the group judging and being judged based on each of our personal criteria. We each had what we considered to be acceptable criteria for ourself. Our personal criteria was arrived at by way of experiences filtering through our personal, and individual personalities. I was not an ideal family member for some of the other members of our group, just as some of them were not ideal for me. We each had our own personal "dogma." Dogma is defined as "a principle, belief, or statement of idea or opinion, especially one formally or authoritatively considered to be absolute truth." The Greek meaning is, "opinion, belief, public, degree from dokein, to seem, to think." We were each operating from our core base of personal dogma, and it didn't consistently or constantly coincide. That doesn't make anyone wrong. It only makes us different!

On the last evening we were scheduled to share a cook-out at the beach. They all wanted steak, and I wanted shrimp. I know it's only my personal perspective, but it seemed obvious to me that the "group" wanted me to "go along" even if I was uncomfortable eating red meat. I felt they wanted me to "go along" in order to be an accepted "acceptable" member of the group. I had spent a lifetime "going along" in order to attempt to win acceptance that never really came as a result of anything external.

I felt disapproval in the air when I maintained my personal preference for shrimp. The staff person responsible for arranging the cook-out had absolutely no problem meeting each of our preferences. So I had shrimp, and I had disapproval from the group. It is so common to see people or groups, in many situations, reject someone just because they have the honest courage to be different. This is a very sad fact, since it inhibits uniqueness and creative expression. Creative expression is life itself; it is God/Love in action.

Following is a poem I wrote a few years
ago.   It seems to custom fit what I am refer-
ring to here.

ME

I like me.   I believe in me.

I feel like me.

I look like me.

I do like me.

I am me.

Sometimes I forget
        to be me,
When I'm afraid
I'm not enough for others.

But then I remember
        that I'm the best me
                I can be; and

Then I'm glad again to be
        ME!

Many wonderful healings happened during the week I spent in Georgia. There were many excellent planned and facilitated exercises. There were tremendous benefits simply from interacting within the group dynamics whether in a formal session or in general activities. We were told to NOT BE ALONE, to do everything with another person present. This component alone helped me spend my fears about being alone and actually seek aloneness so that I could identify and appreciate my personal individualization. By spending a full week, twenty-four hours a day, with the same people I was shown how much I appreciate time with myself. I remembered to be thankful for ME, all by myself. By the sixth day I could not only see value in both individual and group time, but I was highly ready to leave the forced "unitedness" and ready to move out into a world where I could be in charge of my own balance. There were times when a lay-facilitator suggested we (I) adopt her criteria for success, and this helped me commit even more to identifying and standing by my own criteria for happiness.

In Georgia I grew up (emotionally) - by leaps and bounds. Although prior to the accident and the death experience, I had developed very well physically, mentally and spiritually, I needed some catching up in the emotional growth department. Georgia had a major effect on my mind, and therefore on my life. Georgia was one of the processes I am now able to faithfully choose for my own sake, for my own continued improved peace of mind. My inner child was getting confident, and believing in her ability to make wise choices in her own behalf. When I was growing up physically, I lived in many homes and attended over 28 schools before finishing high school. These **experiences** showed me that in life there is a banquet of choices, and we are not the victim of fate. We are merely shown, through physical manifestations what our inner spirit is projecting. We can grab onto what our spirit is currently manifesting in our physical world and enhance it, or we can change our minds and move on to look at other options until we find the best manifestation for our personal specific individualization. Changing our minds is a key phrase here. Changing our "minds" includes changing our subconscious "thinking." To do this we must be willing to go beneath superficial defense mechanisms and reprogram core belief systems. We can do this with a variety of treatment modalities. However the example shared in the chapter called "John" is the modality I have found to be the most expedient, efficient, far reaching, and most profound of all treatment modalities I have engaged in.

I went to Georgia with an open mind, and feeling determined to do whatever was necessary for me to purge old interference and reprogram peace and love in its place. I had the chance to live within a family system similar to the one I grew up in. Through this opportunity I was shown this "one" option again. This helped me redefine more clearly what I wanted instead. I realized that it was safe to dare to be different - to be ME. The last evening in Georgia at the cook-out I quickly sought solitude on the dock looking out over the Atlantic Ocean. I sat alone for several minutes appreciating "my own space." As I sat looking out at the massive and powerful water I felt the truth of our Creator seep into my pores and fill every atom of my existence. After a few deep sighs, I began repeating over and over again, "Forgive them Father for they know not what they do." And as I was saying this, I realized I needed to also say "Forgive me Father for I know not what I do." I continued these statements until I felt total peace. I had let go of the week of mutual judgements. I now saw the mutual judgements brought into balance, and they were simply personal evaluations of choices to paint our individual pictures.

When I rejoined the group we told stories and jokes, and had a laughing good time.

NO JOKE

I'm **not** really a joke teller, but I recently heard a very funny one, so I'd like to share it with you. It requires stuttering, and that's definitely not one of my special talents. So I'll offer my apologies in advance for the lousy stuttering you are about to hear. The story is a about a bible salesman, and it goes like this:

There was a job advertised for a bible salesman, and three men applied. The interviewer asked the first one, "Why do you think you can do a good job for us?" He answered, "Because I am willing to accept all the 'no-s' it will take to get to the 'yes-s'."

"Well," thought the interviewer, "that's the kind of attitude we want." So he told the applicant that he had two others to interview, but he liked this man's attitude so he'd send him off with some bibles and an opportunity to prove himself. "I'm going to let you show me how many bibles you can sell. What do you think you can sell in twenty-four hours?"

"Oh, I can sell twenty bibles in one day alone. I'll show you." the applicant answered.

The next applicant came in, and the interviewer asked him the same question, "Why do you think you can do a good job for us?"

He answered, "Because I'm a positive thinker, and I can visualize myself being your top salesperson."

"Hmm," thought the interviewer, "Visualize, huh? I know that approach works for athletes, I should give him a try."

"I tell you what," the interviewer said to the second applicant, "I'll give you the same opportunity I gave to the first applicant. You have twenty-four hours to show me how many bibles you can sell, and the one who sells the most will get the job."

"Great!" said the second applicant. "I visualize selling fifty bibles."

The third applicant came into the interviewer's office, and the interviewer asked him the same question,"Why do you think you can do a good job for us?"

"B b b b b b b b e c c c cause I wh wh wh wh want to." the third applicant said.

"Oh boy!" thought the interviewer. "What am I going to do? I don't want to be cruel and remark on the man's obvious speech problem. I guess I'll give him the same chance as the others and he'll rule himself out."

"How many bibles do you think you can sell in twenty-four hours?" he asked the applicant.

"Wh wh wh wh wh wh one hu hu hu hundred." he stuttered.

"This guy's dreaming." thought the interviewer with a chuckle. But he sent him off with plenty of bibles and told him to report back in twenty-four hours.

The next day the first applicant came back and reported that he had sold only twelve bibles, but he pleaded for more time. "It only means that I have to be patient and get past more of the 'no-s' before I hit the many 'yes-s'." he said.

"Let me see what the others have done, and I'll let you know," the interviewer answered.

and saying, "I sold forty-six bibles! Very close to my visualization. I'll continue to visualize more and more and my sales will go higher and higher." He was very pleased with himself, so was the interviewer.

"Wow, that's great!" said the interviewer. "I'd like to say that you have the job, but I have to let the third applicant report in first. I'm sure he couldn't possibly have done as well as you have so I'll get back to you."

The third applicant came in and sat down very confidently. The interviewer asked him, "How many bibles did you sell?"

"I so so so so so sold n n n n ninety-f f f f f f f four." he stuttered.

"What?!" thought the interviewer, "how could he?!"

"How did you sell ninety-four bibles in only one day?" asked the interviewer in astonishment.

"I t t t t told th th th them th th th th th th that if th th th th they didn't w w w w w w w want to buy wh wh wh wh wh wh one, I w w w w w w ould read it t t t t t t to th th th them."

When I heard this story I laughed from deep in my belly. I hope you enjoyed a similar response.

The stuttering bible salesman is a beautiful example that the joke doesn't have to me on us. He took whatever he had, even if society called it a handicap, and made excellent use of it. He is successful in creating his own world, and his own results.

I told the story about the bible salesman with my peers in Georgia and the humor was bonding and healing. There was another exercise we participated in the latter part of the week which asked us to "visualize" for our future. In this exercise I began painting MY new picture. At this point I was remembering the Almighty Creator in more of my personal individualization, and I felt powerfully co-creative with the abundant God/Love. I visualized a home, very specifically and ideally. I didn't know how it would become mine, but I knew that a power greater than I, was in charge of that. Within a week after returning home to Michigan I saw the home I wanted. I prayed for a significant sign from the Almighty Creator to show me that this was the best thing for me at this point in time. The sign I got was to have my old house sold in less than twenty-four hours, for the full asking price, and to buyers who already had a mortgage approved. I felt I was being told to "Do it! This is right for you!" I didn't even have a job in the town I was buying into. But I knew it would be taken care of. I am now building my private practice in the beautiful town of Traverse City, Michigan, and loving every minute of it. I feel extremely effective and vital to my community. I feel ALIVE again.

Another visualization I was practicing was for a beautiful open, honest, deeply caring relationship with someone who had interests and perspectives in common with mine. I have that relationship now. It is indescribable. When I express love toward the man in my life, I feel like I am loving myself. The synchronization we consistently feel is truly a manifestation of the Almighty Creator: LOVE. My picture, my life, is being repainted, beautifully. My oldest daughter and her mate have moved in with us, and we are really enjoying each others company as adults now. It's wonderful, and it's healthy. We communicate openly and honestly with each of us owning our own positions, needs, and desires. We are doing this with great respect for each other while also respecting the fact that we don't always agree. And that's perfectly o.k. My youngest daughter and I are emotionally closer than we ever were before. I also have a new teenager in my life to love and share with, when she'll let me.

She is my husband's daughter. Life is as
beautiful as you can allow yourself to dream it
to be. We have the responsibility to make
choices in our own behalf. I wrote the following poem several years ago.

RESPONSIBILITY

Responsibility is

> the ability to

> respond.

Choose a response

> within your abilities.

Accept it.

Expand your abilities:
> expand your options.

Expand your responses.

Enjoy your Response Ability!

I remember that I am a piece of the Almighty Creator being expressed into life. My truth is LOVE. I am a spiritual being having a human experience ...

I AM

Born ... a babe, full of life

I AM!

Growing, reaching for adulthood and autonomy,

I AM!

Learning, for future use,

I AM!

Suffering, the trials of adolescence,

I AM!

Maturing, making commitments,

I AM!

Experiencing love, joy, and accomplishment,

I AM!

Surviving loss, disappointment, grief,
      rejection, and change,

But still, I AM!

I am not only
      a job, spouse, parent, friend, helper,
      giver, taker, sharer

I AM ME! - Beautiful ME!
      all that I am born to be!

VICTORIA

"Hello, Vicky?" I asked.

"Yes." she said simply.

"This is Dr. Mary McMurray, my answering service said you called and that you've had a heart attack. Are you alright?" I went on quickly and with concern.

"Oh Mary! I'm so glad you called. I've called all over the state trying to get your new phone number. I'm fine. I'm great. I had a heart attack. But I'm fine." she was saying excitedly.

"What happened?"

"The heart attack was nothing. Well, not nothing, but something else is bigger."

Vicky went on to tell me about her near-death-experience.

Some of Vicky's remarks were:

They told me I was in a coma. But I was there all the time.

I really saw the light! It was great! It was better than a hundred orgasms all at once.

I'm not afraid of anything anymore. I'm really standing up for myself these days.

I felt completely loved! It was a deep warm feeling.

They told me that I had four personalities when I first came back - but they're wrong - I have 32, or more personalities. I can be anything I want!

I'm not afraid to die now. It's beautiful! Coming back isn't easy, but I can see how I can express myself more fully in life now, and without being afraid.

Everyone thinks I'm crazy when I talk about what happened. Is it only people who have experienced it who can understand?

I listened to Victoria tell me, very excitedly, about her experience and it took me back to my own experience again. I was thankful that she had tracked me down. I embraced the lovely feelings she conjured for me with her story, and then I said, "I'm so happy for you Victoria." I was thrilled that she too had been given a glimpse of the truth of love.

The truth lives within each and everyone one of us, and we don't have to die to remember it. LOVE!

TOEVER

Together Forever
Infinitely United
Soul to Soul

Saturated with
Serenity

Basking in Love.

ORDER FORM

TOEVER Items:

T-Shirts $14.50
100% cotton, X-L

Key Chains $ 2.25
Glow in Dark-Gold

BOOKS:

I DIED TO REMEMBER, Softcover $ 9.95

TAKING CHARGE
        IN A CHANGING WORLD $29.95
    Hardcover/Binder

Mail Order to: **MALLARD PUBLISHING**
                P.O. Box 82-P
                Traverse City, MI 49685-0082

Quantity	Item	Price

Subtotal   _____
Plus Shipping   _____
4% Tax for Mich. _____
TOTAL   _____

Note: Shipping is a minimum of $3.00 or 15%
of the order whichever is GREATER.

Or call 1-800-237-7729 for VISA only.